# Toronto Blue Jays 2020

## A Baseball Companion

*Edited by R.J. Anderson, Craig Goldstein and Bret Sayre*

**Baseball Prospectus**

Craig Brown, Steven Goldman and David Pease, Consultant Editors
Robert Au, Harry Pavlidis and Amy Pircher, Statistics Editors

Copyright © 2020 by DIY Baseball, LLC.
All rights reserved

This book or any part thereof may not be reproduced or transmitted in any form or by any means, electronic or mechanical, including photocopying, recording, or by any information storage and retrieval system, without permission in writing from the publisher.

Limit of Liability/Disclaimer of Warranty: While the publisher and the author have used their best efforts in preparing this book, they make no representations or warranties with respect to the accuracy or completeness of the contents of this book and specifically disclaim any implied warranties of merchantability or fitness for a particular purpose. No warranty may be created or extended by sales representatives or written sales materials. The advice and strategies contained herein may not be suitable for your situation. You should consult with a professional where appropriate. Neither the publisher nor the author shall be liable for any loss of profit or any other commercial damages, including but not limited to special, incidental, consequential, or other damages.

Library of Congress Cataloging-in-Publication Data:
paperback
ISBN-13: 978-1-949332-92-6

Project Credits
Cover Design: Michael Byzewski at Aesthetic Apparatus
Interior Design and Production: Jeff Pease, Dave Pease
Layout: Jeff Pease, Dave Pease

Baseball icon courtesy of Uberux, from https://www.shareicon.net/author/uberux

Ballpark diagram courtesy of Lou Spirito/THIRTY81 Project, https://thirty81project.com/

Manufactured in the United States of America
10 9 8 7 6 5 4 3 2 1

# Table of Contents

Statistical Introduction . . . . . . . . . . . . . . . . . . . . . . . . . . . . . . . . . . . . . . . . . . . . . v

## Part 1: Team Analysis

Toronto Blue Jays: Where Are You Going, Where Have You Been? . . . . . 3
    *Ben Carsley, Keanan Lamb and Matthew Trueblood*

Performance Graphs . . . . . . . . . . . . . . . . . . . . . . . . . . . . . . . . . . . . . . . . . . . . . . 7

2019 Team Performance . . . . . . . . . . . . . . . . . . . . . . . . . . . . . . . . . . . . . . . . . 8

2020 Team Projections . . . . . . . . . . . . . . . . . . . . . . . . . . . . . . . . . . . . . . . . . . 9

Team Personnel . . . . . . . . . . . . . . . . . . . . . . . . . . . . . . . . . . . . . . . . . . . . . . . 10

Rogers Centre Stats . . . . . . . . . . . . . . . . . . . . . . . . . . . . . . . . . . . . . . . . . . . 11

Blue Jays Team Analysis . . . . . . . . . . . . . . . . . . . . . . . . . . . . . . . . . . . . . . . . 13

## Part 2: Player Analysis

Blue Jays Player Analysis . . . . . . . . . . . . . . . . . . . . . . . . . . . . . . . . . . . . . . . 18

Blue Jays Prospects . . . . . . . . . . . . . . . . . . . . . . . . . . . . . . . . . . . . . . . . . . . 101

## Part 3: Featured Articles

The Baseball Is Juiced (Again) . . . . . . . . . . . . . . . . . . . . . . . . . . . . . . . . . . 117
    *Robert Arthur*

The Moral Hazard of Playing It Safe . . . . . . . . . . . . . . . . . . . . . . . . . . . . . 121
    *Craig Goldstein*

Index of Names . . . . . . . . . . . . . . . . . . . . . . . . . . . . . . . . . . . . . . . . . . . . . . . 127

# Statistical Introduction

Sports are, fundamentally, a blend of athletic endeavor and storytelling. Baseball, like any other sport, tells its stories in so many ways: in the arc of a game from the stands or a season from the box scores, in photos, or even in numbers. At Baseball Prospectus, we understand that statistics don't replace observation or any of baseball's stories, but complement everything else that makes the game so much fun.

What stats help us with is with patterns and precision, variance and value. This book can help you learn things you may not see from watching a game or hundred, whether it's the path of a career over time or the breadth of the entire MLB. We'd also never ask you to choose between our numbers and the experience of viewing a game from the cheap seats or the comfort of your home; our publication combines running the numbers with observations and wisdom from some of the brightest minds we can find. But if you *do* want to learn more about the numbers beyond what's on the backs of player jerseys, let us help explain.

## Offense

We've revised our methodology for determining batting value. Long-time readers of the book will notice that we've retired True Average in favor of a new metric: Deserved Runs Created Plus (DRC+). Developed by Jonathan Judge and our stats team, this statistic measures everything a player does at the plate–reaching base, hitting for power, making outs, and moving runners over–and puts it on a scale where 100 equals league-average performance. A DRC+ of 150 is terrific, a DRC+ of 100 is average and a DRC+ of 75 means you better be an excellent defender.

DRC+ also does a better job than any of our previous metrics in taking contextual factors into account. The model adjusts for how the park affects performance, but also for things like the talent of the opposing pitcher, value of different types of batted-ball events, league, temperature and other factors. It's able to describe a player's expected offensive contribution than any other statistic we've found over the years, and also does a better job of predicting future performance as well.

There's a lot more to DRC+'s story, and you can read all about it in greater depth near the end of this book.

Toronto Blue Jays 2020

The other aspect of run-scoring is baserunning, which we quantify using Baserunning Runs. BRR not only records the value of stolen bases (or getting caught in the act), but also accounts for all the stuff that doesn't show up on the back of a baseball card: a runner's ability to go first to third on a single, or advance on a fly ball.

## Defense

Where offensive value is *relatively* easy to identify and understand, defensive value is...not. Over the past dozen years, the sabermetric community has focused mostly on stats based on zone data: a real-live human person records the type of batted ball and estimated landing location, and models are created that give expected outs. From there, you can compare fielders' actual outs to those expected ones. Simple, right?

Unfortunately, zone data has two major issues. First, zone data is recorded by commercial data providers who keep the raw data private unless you pay for it. (All the statistics we build in this book and on our website use public data as inputs.) That hurts our ability to test assumptions or duplicate results. Second, over the years it has become apparent that there's quite a bit of "noise" in zone-based fielding analysis. Sometimes the conclusions drawn from zone data don't hold up to scrutiny, and sometimes the different data provided by different providers don't look anything alike, giving wildly different results. Sometimes the hard-working professional stringers or scorers might unknowingly inflict unconscious bias into the mix: for example good fielders will often be credited with more expected outs despite the data, and ballparks with high press boxes tend to score more line drives than ones with a lower press box.

Enter our Fielding Runs Above Average (FRAA). For most positions, FRAA is built from play-by-play data, which allows us to avoid the subjectivity found in many other fielding metrics. The idea is this: count how many fielding plays are made by a given player and compare that to expected plays for an average fielder at their position (based on pitcher ground ball tendencies and batter handedness). Then we adjust for park and base-out situations.

When it comes to catchers, our methodology is a little different thanks to the laundry list of responsibilities they're tasked with beyond just, well, catching and throwing the ball. By now you've probably heard about "framing" or the art of making umpires more likely to call balls outside the strike zone for strikes. To put this into one tidy number, we incorporate pitch tracking data (for the years it exists) and adjust for important factors like pitcher, umpire, batter and home-field advantage using a mixed-model approach. This grants us a number for how many strikes the catcher is personally adding to (or subtracting from) his pitchers' performance...which we then convert to runs added or lost using linear weights.

Framing is one of the biggest parts of determining catcher value, but we also take into account blocking balls from going past, whether a scorer deems it a passed ball or a wild pitch. We use a similar approach—one that really benefits from the pitch tracking data that tells us what ends up in the dirt and what doesn't. We also include a catcher's ability to prevent stolen bases and how well they field balls in play, and *finally* we come up with our FRAA for catchers.

## Pitching

Both pitching and fielding make up the half of baseball that isn't run scoring: run prevention. Separating pitching from fielding is a tough task, and most recent pitching analysis has branched off from Voros McCracken's famous (and controversial) statement, "There is little if any difference among major-league pitchers in their ability to prevent hits on balls hit in the field of play." The research of the analytic community has validated this to some extent, and there are a host of "defense-independent" pitching measures that have been developed to try and extract the effect of the defense behind a hurler from the pitcher's work.

Our solution to this quandary is Deserved Run Average (DRA), our core pitching metric. DRA looks like earned run average (ERA), the tried-and-true pitching stat you've seen on every baseball broadcast or box score from the past century, but it's very different. To start, DRA takes an event-by-event look at what the pitchers does, and adjusts the value of that event based on different environmental factors like park, batter, catcher, umpire, base-out situation, run differential, inning, defense, home field advantage, pitcher role and temperature. That mixed model gives us a pitcher's expected contribution, similar to what we do for our DRC+ model for hitters and FRAA model for catchers. (Oh, and we also consider the pitcher's effect on basestealing and on balls getting past the catcher.)

It's important to note that DRA is set to the scale of runs allowed per nine innings (RA9) instead of ERA, which makes DRA's scale slightly higher than ERA's. The reason for this is because ERA tends to overrate three types of pitchers:

1. Pitchers who play in parks where scorers hand out more errors. Official scorers differ significantly in the frequency at which they assign errors to fielders.
2. Ground-ball pitchers, because a substantial proportion of errors occur on groundballs.
3. Pitchers who aren't very good. Better pitchers often allow fewer unearned runs than bad pitchers, because good pitchers tend to find ways to get out of jams.

Since the last time you picked up an edition of this book, we've also made a few minor changes to DRA to make it better. Recent research into "tunneling"—the act of throwing consecutive pitches that appear similar from a batter's point of view until after the swing decision point–data has given us a new contextual factor to account for in DRA: plate distance. This refers to the distance between successive pitches as they approach the plate, and while it has a smaller effect than factors like velocity or whiff rate, it still can help explain pitcher strikeout rate in our model.

## New Pitching Metrics for 2020

We're including a few "new" pitching metrics in the book for the 2020 edition, though unlike last year, these numbers may be a little bit more familiar to those of you who have spent some time investigating baseball statistics.

### Fastball Percentage

Our fastball percentage (FB%) statistic measures how frequently a pitcher throws a pitch classified as a "fastball," measured as a percentage of overall pitches thrown. We qualify three types of fastballs:

1. The traditional four-seam fastball;
2. The two-seam fastball or sinker;
3. "Hard cutters," which are pitches that have the movement profile of a cut fastball and are used as the pitcher's primary offering or in place of a more traditional fastball.

For example, a pitcher with a FB% of 67 throws any combination of these three pitches about two-thirds of the time.

### Whiff Rate

Everybody loves a swing and a miss, and whiff rate (WHF) measures how frequently pitchers induce a swinging strike. To calculate WHF, we add up all the pitches thrown that ended with a swinging strike, then divide that number by a pitcher's total pitches thrown. Most often, high whiff rates correlate with high strikeout rates (and overall effective pitcher performance).

### Called Strike Probability

Called Strike Probability (CSP) is a number that represents the likelihood that all of a pitcher's pitches will be called a strike while controlling for location, pitcher and batter handedness, umpire and count. Here's how it works: on each pitch, our model determines how many times (out of 100) that a similar pitch was called for a strike given those factors mentioned above, and when normalized for each batter's strike zone. Then we average the CSP for all pitches thrown by a pitcher in a season, and that gives us the yearly CSP percentage you see in the stats boxes.

As you might imagine, pitchers with a higher CSP are more likely to work in the zone, where pitchers with a lower CSP are likely locating their pitches outside the normal strike zone, for better or for worse.

## Projections

Many of you aren't turning to this book just for a look at what a player has done, but for a look at what a player is going to do: the PECOTA projections. PECOTA, initially developed by Nate Silver (who has moved on to greater fame as a political analyst), consists of three parts:

1. Major-league equivalencies, which use minor-league statistics to project how a player will perform in the major leagues;
2. Baseline forecasts, which use weighted averages and regression to the mean to estimate a player's current true talent level; and
3. Aging curves, which uses the career paths of comparable players to estimate how a player's statistics are likely to change over time.

With all those important things covered, let's take a look at what's in the book this year.

## Team Prospectus

Most of this book is composed of team chapters, with one for each of the 30 major-league franchises. On the first page of each chapter, you'll see a box that contains some of the key statistics for each team as well as a very inviting stadium diagram. (You can see an example of this for the Milwaukee Brewers on this very page!)

We start with the team name, their unadjusted 2019 win-loss record, and their divisional ranking. Beneath that are a host of other team statistics. **Pythag** presents an adjusted 2019 winning percentage, calculated by taking runs scored per game (**RS/G**) and runs allowed per game (**RA/G**) for the team, and running them through a version of Bill James' Pythagorean formula that was refined and improved by David Smyth and Brandon Heipp. (The formula is called "Pythagenpat," which is equally fun to type and to say.)

Next up is **DRC+**, described earlier, to indicate the overall hitting ability of the team either above or below league-average. Run prevention on the pitching side is covered by **DRA** (also mentioned earlier) and another metric: Fielding Independent Pitching (**FIP**), which calculates another ERA-like statistic based on strikeouts, walks, and home runs recorded. Defensive Efficiency Rating (**DER**) tells us the percentage of balls in play turned into outs for the team, and is a quick fielding shorthand that rounds out run prevention.

After that, we have several measures related to roster composition, as opposed to on-field performance. **B-Age** and **P-Age** tell us the average age of a team's batters and pitchers, respectively. **Salary** is the combined team payroll for all on-field players, and Doug Pappas' Marginal Dollars per Marginal Win (**M$/MW**) tells us how much money a team spent to earn production above replacement level.

Ending this batch of statistics is the number of disabled list days a team had over the season (**IL Days**) and the amount of salary paid to players on the disabled list (**$ on IL**); this final number is expressed as a percentage of total payroll.

Next to each of these stats, we've listed each team's MLB rank in that category from first to 30th. In this, first always indicates a positive outcome and 30th a negative outcome, except in the case of salary—first is highest.

After the franchise statistics, we share a few items about the team's home ballpark. There's the aforementioned diagram of the park's dimensions (including distances to the outfield wall), a graphic showing the height of the wall from the left-field pole to the right-field pole, and a table showing three-year park factors for the stadium. The park factors are displayed as indexes where 100 is average, 110 means that the park inflates the statistic in question by 10 percent, and 90 means that the park deflates the statistic in question by 10 percent.

On the second page of each team chapter, you'll find three graphs. The first is the **2019 Hit List Ranking**. This shows our Hit List Rank for the team on each day of the 2019 season and is intended to give you a picture of the ups and downs of the team's season. Hit List Rank measures overall team performance and drives the Hit List Power Rankings at the baseballprospectus.com website.

The second graph is **Committed Payroll** and helps you see how the team's payroll has compared to the MLB and divisional average payrolls over time. Payroll figures are current as of January 1, 2020; with so many free agents still unsigned as of this writing, the final 2020 figure will likely be significantly different for many teams. (In the meantime, you can always find the most current data at Baseball Prospectus' Cot's Baseball Contracts page.)

The third graph is **Farm System Ranking** and displays how the Baseball Prospectus prospect team has ranked the organization's farm system since 2007.

After the graphs, we have a **Personnel** section that lists many of the important decision-makers and upper-level field and operations staff members for the franchise, as well as any former Baseball Prospectus staff members who are currently part of the organization. (In very rare circumstances, someone might be on both lists!)

## Juan Soto  LF

Born: 10/25/98  Age: 21  Bats: L  Throws: L
Height: 6'1"  Weight: 185  Origin: International Free Agent, 2015

| YEAR | TEAM | LVL | AGE | PA  | R   | 2B | 3B | HR | RBI | BB  | K   | SB | CS | AVG/OBP/SLG    |
|------|------|-----|-----|-----|-----|----|----|----|-----|-----|-----|----|----|----------------|
| 2017 | NAT  | RK  | 18  | 27  | 3   | 1  | 1  | 0  | 4   | 2   | 1   | 0  | 0  | .320/.370/.440 |
| 2017 | HAG  | A   | 18  | 96  | 15  | 5  | 0  | 3  | 14  | 10  | 8   | 1  | 2  | .360/.427/.523 |
| 2018 | HAG  | A   | 19  | 74  | 12  | 5  | 3  | 5  | 24  | 14  | 13  | 2  | 0  | .373/.486/.814 |
| 2018 | POT  | A+  | 19  | 73  | 17  | 3  | 1  | 7  | 18  | 11  | 8   | 0  | 1  | .371/.466/.790 |
| 2018 | HAR  | AA  | 19  | 35  | 4   | 2  | 0  | 2  | 10  | 4   | 7   | 1  | 0  | .323/.400/.581 |
| 2018 | WAS  | MLB | 19  | 494 | 77  | 25 | 1  | 22 | 70  | 79  | 99  | 5  | 2  | .292/.406/.517 |
| 2019 | WAS  | MLB | 20  | 659 | 110 | 32 | 5  | 34 | 110 | 108 | 132 | 12 | 1  | .282/.401/.548 |
| 2020 | WAS  | MLB | 21  | 630 | 92  | 30 | 3  | 35 | 102 | 85  | 123 | 5  | 2  | .284/.382/.543 |

Comparables: Ronald Acuña Jr., Mike Trout, Tony Conigliaro

| YEAR | TEAM | LVL | AGE | PA  | DRC+ | VORP | BABIP | BRR  | FRAA                    | WARP |
|------|------|-----|-----|-----|------|------|-------|------|-------------------------|------|
| 2017 | NAT  | RK  | 18  | 27  | 135  | 1.5  | .333  | 0.0  | RF(9): -1.1             | 0.0  |
| 2017 | HAG  | A   | 18  | 96  | 181  | 8.0  | .373  | 1.0  | RF(19): -1.9, LF(2): -0.3 | 0.9  |
| 2018 | HAG  | A   | 19  | 74  | 222  | 14.5 | .405  | 0.3  | RF(14): 1.1, CF(2): 0.2 | 1.2  |
| 2018 | POT  | A+  | 19  | 73  | 260  | 15.4 | .340  | 1.4  | RF(14): 1.0, LF(1): 0.0 | 1.6  |
| 2018 | HAR  | AA  | 19  | 35  | 113  | 3.6  | .364  | 0.0  | LF(4): 0.6, RF(4): -0.5 | 0.1  |
| 2018 | WAS  | MLB | 19  | 494 | 125  | 40.5 | .338  | -0.5 | LF(114): 2.7            | 3.0  |
| 2019 | WAS  | MLB | 20  | 659 | 136  | 49.0 | .312  | 1.4  | LF(150): -0.8           | 4.9  |
| 2020 | WAS  | MLB | 21  | 630 | 133  | 43.6 | .310  | -0.1 | LF 3                    | 4.8  |

## Position Players

After all that information and a thoughtful bylined essay covering each team, we present our player comments. These are also bylined, but due to frequent franchise shifts during the offseason, our bylines are more a rough guide than a perfect accounting of who wrote what.

Each player is listed with the major-league team that employed him as of early January 2020. If a player changed teams after that point via free agency, trade, or any other method, you'll be able to find them in the chapter for their previous squad.

As an example, take a look at the player comment for Nationals outfielder Juan Soto: the stat block that accompanies his written comment is at the top of this page. First we cover biographical information (age is as of June 30, 2020) before moving onto the stats themselves. Our statistic columns include standard identifying information like **YEAR**, **TEAM**, **LVL** (level of affiliated play) and **AGE** before getting into the numbers. Next, we provide raw, untranslated numbers like you might find on the back of your dad's baseball cards: **PA** (plate appearances), **R** (runs), **2B** (doubles), **3B** (triples), **HR** (home runs), **RBI** (runs batted in), **BB** (walks), **K** (strikeouts), **SB** (stolen bases) and **CS** (caught stealing).

Next, we have unadjusted "slash" statistics: **AVG** (batting average), **OBP** (on-base percentage) and **SLG** (slugging percentage). Following the slash line is **DRC+** (Deserved Runs Created Plus), which we described earlier as total offensive expected contribution compared to the league average.

One of our oldest active metrics, **VORP** (Value Over Replacement Player), considers offensive production, position and plate appearances. In essence, it is the number of runs contributed beyond what a replacement-level player at the same position would contribute if given the same percentage of team plate appearances. VORP does not consider the quality of a player's defense.

**BABIP** (batting average on balls in play) tells us how often a ball in play fell for a hit, and can help us identify whether a batter may have been lucky or not…but note that high BABIPs also tend to follow the great hitters of our time, as well as speedy singles hitters who put the ball on the ground.

The next item is **BRR** (Baserunning Runs), which covers all of a player's baserunning accomplishments including (but not limited to) swiped bags and failed attempts. Next is **FRAA** (Fielding Runs Above Average), which also includes the number of games previously played at each position noted in parentheses. Multi-position players have only their two most frequent positions listed here, but their total FRAA number reflects all positions played.

Our last column here is **WARP** (Wins Above Replacement Player). WARP estimates the total value of a player, which means for hitters it takes into account hitting runs above average (calculated using the DRC+ model), BRR and FRAA. Then, it makes an adjustment for positions played and gives the player a credit for plate appearances based upon the difference between "replacement level"—which is derived from the quality of players added to a team's roster after the start of the season–and the league average.

The final line just below the stats box is **PECOTA** data, which is discussed further in a following section.

## Catchers

Catchers are a special breed, and thus they have earned their own separate box which displays some of the defensive metrics that we've built just for them. As an example, let's check out J.T. Realmuto.

The **YEAR** and **TEAM** columns match what you'd find in the other stat box. **P. COUNT** indicates the number of pitches thrown while the catcher was behind the plate, including swinging strikes, fouls and balls in play. **FRM RUNS** is the total run value the catcher provided (or cost) his team by influencing the umpire to call strikes where other catchers did not. **BLK RUNS** expresses the total run value above or below average for the catcher's ability to prevent wild pitches and passed balls. **THRW RUNS** is calculated using a similar model as the previous two statistics, and it measures a catcher's ability to throw out basestealers but also to dissuade them from testing his arm in the first place. It takes into account factors like the pitcher (including his delivery and pickoff move) and baserunner (who could be as fast as Billy Hamilton or as slow as Yonder Alonso). **TOT RUNS** is the sum of all of the previous three statistics.

## Justin Verlander   RHP
Born: 02/20/83   Age: 37   Bats: R   Throws: R
Height: 6'5"   Weight: 225   Origin: Round 1, 2004 Draft (#2 overall)

| YEAR | TEAM | LVL | AGE | W | L | SV | G | GS | IP | H | HR | BB/9 | K/9 | K | GB% | BABIP |
|---|---|---|---|---|---|---|---|---|---|---|---|---|---|---|---|---|
| 2017 | DET | MLB | 34 | 10 | 8 | 0 | 28 | 28 | 172 | 153 | 23 | 3.5 | 9.2 | 176 | 34% | .283 |
| 2017 | HOU | MLB | 34 | 5 | 0 | 0 | 5 | 5 | 34 | 17 | 4 | 1.3 | 11.4 | 43 | 32% | .194 |
| 2018 | HOU | MLB | 35 | 16 | 9 | 0 | 34 | 34 | 214 | 156 | 28 | 1.6 | 12.2 | 290 | 31% | .272 |
| 2019 | HOU | MLB | 36 | 21 | 6 | 0 | 34 | 34 | 223 | 137 | 36 | 1.7 | 12.1 | 300 | 36% | .219 |
| 2020 | HOU | MLB | 37 | 15 | 6 | 0 | 29 | 29 | 184 | 138 | 28 | 2.3 | 12.1 | 248 | 35% | .274 |

Comparables: Zack Greinke, A.J. Burnett, Aníbal Sánchez

| YEAR | TEAM | LVL | AGE | WHIP | ERA | DRA | WARP | MPH | FB% | WHF | CSP |
|---|---|---|---|---|---|---|---|---|---|---|---|
| 2017 | DET | MLB | 34 | 1.28 | 3.82 | 4.03 | 3.0 | 97.7 | 58 | 11 | 47.8 |
| 2017 | HOU | MLB | 34 | 0.65 | 1.06 | 3.08 | 0.9 | 97.5 | 59.6 | 15.1 | 49.9 |
| 2018 | HOU | MLB | 35 | 0.90 | 2.52 | 2.33 | 7.3 | 97.5 | 61.2 | 16.2 | 51.6 |
| 2019 | HOU | MLB | 36 | 0.80 | 2.58 | 2.51 | 7.9 | 96.8 | 49.9 | 17.5 | 48.3 |
| 2020 | HOU | MLB | 37 | 1.01 | 2.75 | 2.95 | 5.3 | 95.8 | 54.6 | 15.1 | 48.2 |

## Pitchers

Let's give our pitchers a turn, using 2019 AL Cy Young winner Justin Verlander as our example. Take a look at his stat block: the first line and the **YEAR**, **TEAM**, **LVL** and **AGE** columns are the same as in the position player example earlier.

Here too, we have a series of columns that display raw, unadjusted statistics compiled by the pitcher over the course of a season: **W** (wins), **L** (losses), **SV** (saves), **G** (games pitched), **GS** (games started), **IP** (innings pitched), **H** (hits allowed) and **HR** (home runs allowed). Next we have two statistics that are rates: **BB/9** (walks per nine innings) and **K/9** (strikeouts per nine innings), before returning to the unadjusted K (strikeouts).

Next up is **GB%** (ground ball percentage), which is the percentage of all batted balls that were hit on the ground, including both outs and hits. Remember, this is based on observational data and subject to human error, so please approach this with a healthy dose of skepticism.

**BABIP** (batting average on balls in play) is calculated using the same methodology as it is for position players, but it often tells us more about a pitcher than it does a hitter. With pitchers, a high BABIP is often due to poor defense or bad luck, and can often be an indicator of potential rebound, and a low BABIP may be cause to expect performance regression. (A typical league-average BABIP is close to .290-.300.)

Toronto Blue Jays 2020

The metrics **WHIP** (walks plus hits per inning pitched) and **ERA** (earned run average) are old standbys: WHIP measures walks and hits allowed on a per-inning basis, while ERA measures earned runs on a nine-inning basis. Neither of these stats are translated or adjusted.

**DRA** (Deserved Run Average) was described at length earlier, and measures how many runs the pitcher "deserved" to allow per nine innings. Please note that since we lack all the data points that would make for a "real" DRA for minor-league events, the DRA displayed for minor league partial-seasons is based off of different data. (That data is a modified version of our cFIP metric, which you can find more information about on our website.)

Just like with hitters, **WARP** (Wins Above Replacement Player) is a total value metric that puts pitchers of all stripes on the same scale as position players. We use DRA as the primary input for our calculation of WARP. You might notice that relief pitchers (due to their limited innings) may have a lower WARP than you were expecting or than you might see in other WARP-like metrics. WARP does not take leverage into account, just the actions a pitcher performs and the expected value of those actions...which ends up judging high-leverage relief pitchers differently than you might imagine given their prestige and market value.

**MPH** gives you the pitcher's 95th percentile velocity for the noted season, in order to give you an idea of what the *peak* fastball velocity a pitcher possesses. Since this comes from our pitch-tracking data, it is not publicly available for minor-league pitchers.

Finally, we display the three new pitching metrics we described earlier. **FB%** (fastball percentage) gives you the percentage of fastballs thrown out of all pitches. **WHF** (whiff rate) tells you the percentage of swinging strikes induced out of all pitches. **CSP** (called strike probability) expresses the likelihood of all pitches thrown to result in a called strike, after controlling for factors like handedness, umpire, pitch type, count and location.

## PECOTA

All players have PECOTA projections for 2020, as well as a set of other numbers that describe the performance of comparable players according to PECOTA. All projections for 2020 are for the player at the date we went to press in early January and are projected into the league and park context as indicated by the team abbreviation. (Note that players at very low levels of the minors are too unpredictable to assess using these numbers.) All PECOTA projected statistics represent a player's projected major-league performance.

Below the projections are the player's three highest-scoring comparable players as determined by PECOTA. All comparables represent a snapshot of how the listed player was performing at the same age as the current player, so if a

23-year-old pitcher is compared to Bartolo Colón, he's actually being compared to a 23-year-old Colón, not the version that pitched for the Rangers in 2018, nor to Colón's career as a whole.

A few points about pitcher projections. First, we aren't yet projecting peak velocity, so that column will be blank in the PECOTA lines. Second, projecting DRA is trickier than evaluating past performance, because it is unclear how deserving each pitcher will be of his anticipated outcomes. However, we know that another DRA-related statistic–contextual FIP or cFIP-estimates future run scoring very well. So for PECOTA, the projected DRA figures you see are based on the past cFIPs generated by the pitcher and comparable players over time, along with the other factors described above.

## Lineouts

In each chapter's Lineouts section, you'll find abbreviated text comments, as well as all the same information you'd find in our full player comments. The only difference is that we limit the stats boxes in this section to only including the 2019 information for each player.

## Managers

After all those wonderful team chapters, we've got statistics for each big-league manager, all of whom are organized by alphabetical order. Here you'll find a block including an extraordinary amount of information collected from each manager's entire career. For more information on the acronyms and what they mean, please visit the Glossary at www.baseballprospectus.com.

There is one important metric that we'd like to call attention to, and you'll find it next to each manager's name: **wRM+** (weighted reliever management plus). Developed by Rob Arthur and Rian Watt, wRM+ investigates how good a manager is at using their best relievers during the moments of highest leverage, using both our proprietary DRA metric as well as Leverage Index. wRM+ is scaled to a league average of 100, and a wRM+ of 105 indicates that relievers were used approximately five percent "better" than average. On the other hand, a wRM+ of 95 would tell us the team used its relievers five percent "worse" than the average team.

While wRM+ does not have an extremely strong correlation with a manager, it is statistically significant; this means that a manager is not *entirely* responsible for a team's wRM+, but does have some effect on that number.

## PECOTA Leaderboards

If you're familiar with PECOTA, then you'll have noticed that the projection system often appears bullish on players coming off a bad year and bearish on players coming off a good year. (This is because the system weights several previous seasons, not just the most recent one.) In addition, we publish the 50th

## Toronto Blue Jays 2020

percentile projections for each player–which is smack in the middle of the range of projected production—which tends to mean PECOTA stat lines don't often have extreme results like 40 home runs or 250 strikeouts in a given season. In essence, PECOTA doesn't project very many extreme seasons.

At the end of the book, we've ranked the top players at each position based on their PECOTA projections. This might help you visualize just how a given player's projection compares to that of their peers, so that even if a dramatic stat line isn't projected, you can still imagine how they stack up against the rest of the league.

# Part 1: Team Analysis

# Toronto Blue Jays: Where Are You Going, Where Have You Been?

Ben Carsley, Keanan Lamb and Matthew Trueblood

**2019: What went Right**

With Vladimir Guerrero Jr., Bo Bichette, and, to an extent, Cavan Biggio, the Jays were selling their fans not on the competitive possibilities of 2019 but on the sons of yesterday's game serving as the pillars of a brighter tomorrow. At some point, they were going to come up and mash. Anything else that happened to the 2019 Blue Jays would be mostly irrelevant.

Fortunately, those prospect debuts went pretty well. Interestingly, it was not Vladito who truly took the league by storm in his first full season, but Bichette. Despite not getting the call until late July (in part due to injury), Bichette flourished, hitting .311/.358/.571 with a 109 DRC+ in 212 PA. With more playing time, he might have challenged for AL Rookie of the Year. Guerrero Jr., the prohibitive favorite to win that award before the season began, had a solid debut as well. He may not be Prime Miguel Cabrera yet, but Jays fans should be happy with a 101 DRC+ and a thrilling Home Run Derby performance from their chonky star-in-the-making.

Biggio performed at about a league-average level despite his eyesore of a batting average due to his excellent batting eye. His 16.5 percent walk rate was roughly equal to that of Juan Soto and his 4.34 pitches seen per plate appearance, had he had enough playing time to qualify, would have placed him between Yasmani Grandal and Max Muncy. The third-most promising season from a young Blue Jay came from a different source: Lourdes Gurriel Jr. The second-year player may not be a future superstar, but he showed great improvement, with 20 home runs in just 314 at-bats. That gives the Blue Jays four young everyday players to build around, whom all project between average starters to superstars. It's also far too early to rule out a long and productive career for Danny Jansen, who struggled at the plate as almost all young catchers do, but also posted positive framing and FRAA numbers. Count him as part of the core, too.

In addition, Ken Giles was good! Reese McGuire showed a pulse! And Jays fans don't have to worry about Aaron Sanchez's blisters anymore. And, uh, OK we're just about out of positives.

## 2019: What Went Wrong

Let's not let the offense completely off the hook. There are some promising youngsters here, yes, but some sore spots as well. Randal Grichuk's five-year extension is even more inexplicable now than it was in April—it takes a very special player to demonstrate that one can hit 31 home runs and still be at the replacement level (a low on-base percentage and bad defense will do that). Neither Rowdy Tellez nor Teoscar Hernández did a thing to grab hold of a permanent spot on this roster, and post-prospect fliers like Brandon Drury, Derek Fisher, and Billy McKinney all flopped.

Still, any woes the Blue Jays experienced at the plate pale in comparison to the performances they received on the mound. Toronto had the third-worst DRA in the majors at a cool 5.78, just barely ahead of the Royals and Mariners. Now that the Jays are also without Sanchez and Marcus Stroman, there's an argument to be made that Toronto has the least starting pitching talent of any team. Matt Shoemaker tore his ACL in April, and by the Blue Jays' standards he had a pretty good season. Trent Thornton had a DRA of 6.08 in 29 starts. Jacob Waguespack was much better; his DRA was only 4.66. By the end of the season, the Jays' most effective starter was 29-year-old journeyman Wilmer Font, making "Comic Sans" an especially apt nickname for this congeries of talent.

It's not uncommon to see a rebuilding team run out retreads and Quad-A guys in their rotation. What's less common, even among basement-dwellers, is the utter lack of hope, either in the present or on the horizon. Starting prospect Sean Reid-Foley was atrocious in both Triple-A and the big leagues. Nate Pearson's upside is matched by his injury risk. At this point, Toronto's safest bet for a homegrown starter who can throw 150-plus innings may be T.J. Zeuch, who largely projects as a back-end starter at best. It seems odd to complain about a shortfall of young pitching talent given the position players the Blue Jays unleashed in 2019, but baseball is demanding that way. —*Ben Carsley*

## Prospect Outlook

When you graduate the likes of Guerrero, Bichette, Biggio, and Jansen (among others) the cupboard is going to look a little empty. There is, however, still much to look forward to. Known for having one of the biggest scouting departments in the game, the Jays definitely do their homework and have a track record for being forward-thinking on the player development side. Next in line to break into the big leagues is big righty **Nate Pearson**. Consistently eclipsing the 160 kph mark on his fastball (that's 99 mph for all you non-Canadians), he managed to break the 100-inning mark for the first time last season, dominating three levels of competition. Don't be surprised if he begins 2020 in High-A Dunedin, where the club traditionally keeps their best prospects to open the season instead of their cold-weather affiliates, but an eventual promotion to the big leagues would not be out of the question.

Much further down the developmental track is infielder **Jordan Groshans**, who has done nothing but mash since being drafted, but lost most of his 2019 season due to a foot injury. A gaggle of pitchers, including first round pick **Alek Manoah**, international bonus baby **Eric Pardinho**, and trade pickup **Simeon Woods Richardson** are all too far away to expect near-term contributions from them even with the Jays having one of the worst rotations in baseball. *—Keanan Lamb*

## 2020 Outlook

The way 2019 unfolded made things easy on Ross Atkins and company. Their work was cut out for them: they needed almost an entirely new starting rotation. Now, they have one. Signing Tanner Roark and trading for Chase Anderson were savvy, value-conscious moves of the type to which Atkins has made Blue Jays fans accustomed. Shun Yamaguchi is a helpful swing man, and because the trend lately is toward (perhaps undue) skepticism toward Japanese players coming over to the majors, Yamaguchi's price tag produced no sticker shock at all.

Hyun-Jin Ryu, however, is something different. That the Blue Jays were willing to guarantee him five years, and that they were able to sell him on their organization even in the depths of the rebuild, is both surprising and encouraging. Ryu's command and control are good enough to make up for his lack of power, and the depth of his repertoire ensures that his decline will be as gentle as his body allows. The big red flag is that body, of course, which has only intermittently allowed him to shoulder starter workloads, but the Jays had to take a risk in order to effect necessary change, and the payoff for this gamble could be well worth it.

The next project will be cobbling together a deeper lineup. As impressive as the rookies were in 2019, there weren't enough of them to cover up the discouraging results of the veterans. His offseason budget directed toward pitching, Atkins bought low on Travis Shaw and Joe Panik. Otherwise, the team will run back many of the tantalizing, youngish projects they've picked up over the last few years—but the deep flaws of those players, like Grichuk and Hernández and Fisher, are starting to overshadow their tools and they won't be youngish much longer. That's the dirty little secret of an immersive rebuild:

## Toronto Blue Jays 2020

The countdown clock to the next rebuild usually begins before the one you're working on is even complete. Ryu is a crucial signing, because the Jays need to get busy winning and sooner than they think. —*Matthew Trueblood*

# Performance Graphs

### *2019 Hit List Ranking*

### *Committed Payroll (in millions)*

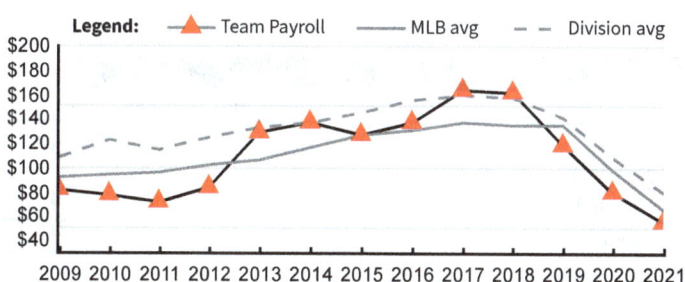

### *Farm System Ranking*

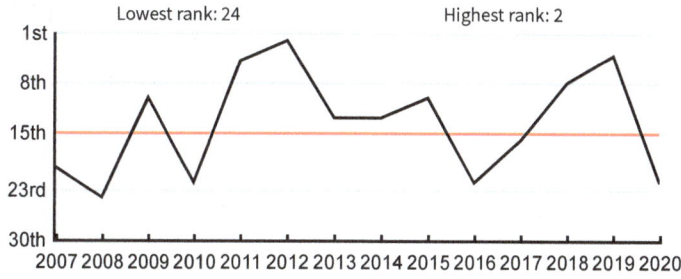

# 2019 Team Performance

### ACTUAL STANDINGS

| Team | W | L | Pct |
|---|---|---|---|
| NYA | 103 | 59 | 0.636 |
| TBA | 96 | 66 | 0.593 |
| BOS | 84 | 78 | 0.519 |
| **TOR** | **67** | **95** | **0.414** |
| BAL | 54 | 108 | 0.333 |

### THIRD-ORDER STANDINGS

| Team | W | L | Pct |
|---|---|---|---|
| TBA | 99 | 63 | 0.613 |
| NYA | 96 | 66 | 0.590 |
| BOS | 88 | 74 | 0.544 |
| **TOR** | **66** | **96** | **0.410** |
| BAL | 59 | 103 | 0.363 |

### TOP HITTERS

| Player | WARP |
|---|---|
| Teoscar Hernández | 2.4 |
| Danny Jansen | 2.2 |
| Cavan Biggio | 2.1 |

### TOP PITCHERS

| Player | WARP |
|---|---|
| Marcus Stroman | 2.8 |
| Ken Giles | 1.6 |
| Sam Gaviglio | 1.3 |

### VITAL STATISTICS

| Statistic Name | Value | Rank |
|---|---|---|
| Pythagenpat | .437 | 21st |
| Runs Scored per Game | 4.48 | 23rd |
| Runs Allowed per Game | 5.11 | 20th |
| Deserved Runs Created Plus | 93 | 19th |
| Deserved Run Average | 5.78 | 28th |
| Fielding Independent Pitching | 4.85 | 22nd |
| Defensive Efficiency Rating | .700 | 19th |
| Batter Age | 25.9 | 1st |
| Pitcher Age | 27.7 | 10th |
| Salary | $117.5M | 21st |
| Marginal $ per Marginal Win | $5.7M | 9th |
| Injured List Days | 1492 | 26th |
| $ on IL | 11% | 5th |

# 2020 Team Projections

## PROJECTED STANDINGS

| Team | W | L | Pct | +/- |
|---|---|---|---|---|
| NYA | 99.0 | 63.0 | 0.611 | -4 |
| TBA | 87.3 | 74.7 | 0.539 | -9 |
| BOS | 84.5 | 77.5 | 0.522 | 0 |
| **TOR** | **76.6** | **85.4** | **0.473** | **10** |
| BAL | 62.9 | 99.1 | 0.388 | 9 |

## TOP PROJECTED HITTERS

| Player | WARP |
|---|---|
| Cavan Biggio | 3.5 |
| Reese McGuire | 2.2 |
| Bo Bichette | 2.1 |

## TOP PROJECTED PITCHERS

| Player | WARP |
|---|---|
| Hyun-Jin Ryu | 2.4 |
| Ken Giles | 1.3 |
| Tanner Roark | 1.2 |

## FARM SYSTEM REPORT

| Top Prospect | Number of Top 101 Prospects |
|---|---|
| Nate Pearson, #19 | 3 |

## KEY DEDUCTIONS

| Player | WARP |
|---|---|
| Justin Smoak | 0.4 |
| Luke Maile | 0.3 |
| Ryan Tepera | 0.2 |
| Breyvic Valera | 0.1 |
| Justin Shafer | -0.1 |
| Richard Ureña | -0.2 |

## KEY ADDITIONS

| Player | WARP |
|---|---|
| Hyun-Jin Ryu | 2.4 |
| Travis Shaw | 1.4 |
| Tanner Roark | 1.2 |
| Shun Yamaguchi | 0.5 |
| Nate Pearson | 0.4 |
| Chase Anderson | 0.4 |
| Santiago Espinal | 0.3 |
| Rafael Dolis | 0.1 |
| Riley Adams | 0.0 |
| Thomas Hatch | 0.0 |

# Team Personnel

**President & CEO**
Mark A. Shapiro

**Executive Vice President, Baseball Operations & General Manager**
Ross Atkins

**Senior Vice President, Player Personnel**
Tony Lacava

**Vice President, International Scouting**
Andrew Tinnish

**Assistant General Manager**
Joe Sheehan

**Manager**
Charlie Montoyo

**BP Alumni**
Matt Bishoff

# Rogers Centre Stats

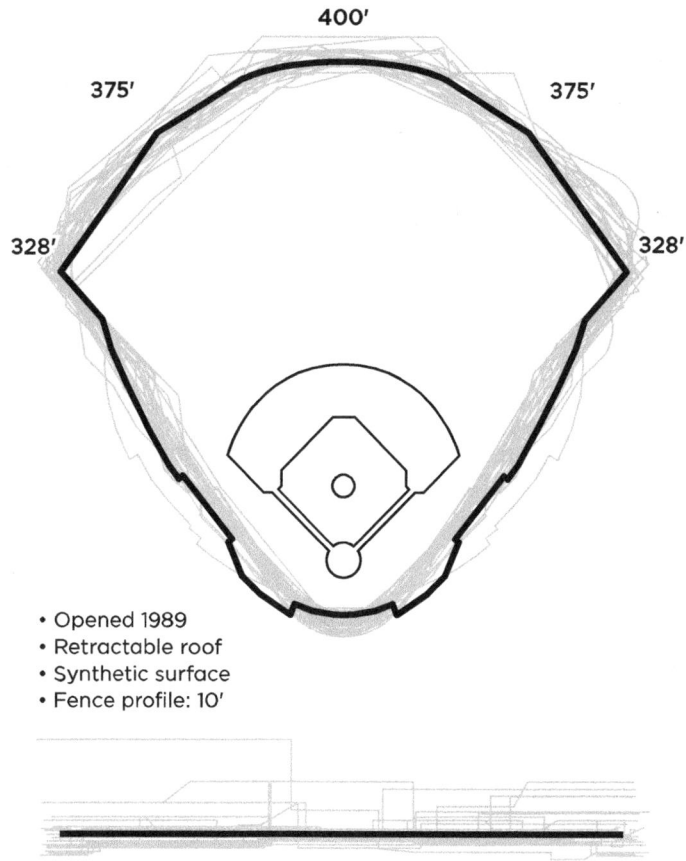

- Opened 1989
- Retractable roof
- Synthetic surface
- Fence profile: 10'

**Three-Year Park Factors**

| Runs | Runs/RH | Runs/LH | HR/RH | HR/LH |
|---|---|---|---|---|
| 99 | 100 | 99 | 107 | 104 |

# Blue Jays Team Analysis

In the bottom of the eighth inning of an otherwise meaningless September game, the 100-win juggernaut New York Yankees inserted Zack Britton to retire the bottom of the 96-loss Toronto Blue Jays' lineup. He did exactly that on 12 pitches, recording a pair of groundouts and a K. It was a routine outing for Britton, a dominant late-inning force, save for one particular moment.

The moment occurred as Britton readied to deliver a pitch to Teoscar Hernández. He came set with his hands held high near his chin, eyes locked on catcher Austin Romine's target. Even without runners on base, he paused in his set position, holding the baseball inside his glove with his left hand. As Britton stood motionless, a monarch butterfly flew over from the first base side of the diamond, coming to rest on his black leather glove.

Breaking his hands from the set position, Britton began his motion to the plate, just as he had more than 9,000 times in his big-league career. This time, however, the butterfly clung to his glove as he did so. The butterfly held on for an instant before fluttering away, presumably intending to put as much space as possible between itself and the hissing nightmare projectile that is a 95 mph big-league sinker. The pitch missed low for ball one to Hernández.

The Blue Jays broadcast crew caught the moment with their center-field camera, playing it back in super-slow motion after the half-inning ended. Calling the game for Rogers' Sportsnet, Dan Shulman insisted "You guys Photoshopped that in there, in the truck!" as his partner Buck Martínez offered his trademark guffaw: "That was awesome."

Later in the same game, the YES broadcast cameras caught a monarch at rest on an unidentified glove. The Blue Jays official Twitter account also shared video captured pregame, when several young Blue Jays were entertained by a butterfly involving itself in their pregame stretch by settling onto Vladimir Guerrero Jr.'s pant leg. Butterflies dominated the night.

Oddly, this was typical for Blue Jays home games in 2019. Butterflies were regularly spotted in the foreground of standard center-field camera shots by members of the viewing public inclined to notice such things. An anecdotal increase in on-field butterfly sightings is supported by observed science across North America: last year was a good one for monarch butterflies.

## Toronto Blue Jays 2020

It was supposed to be a good year for prospects in Toronto, too.

Even though he raced to the big leagues at 21, Bo Bichette's progress through the minors was marked by a specific pattern: a short, post-promotion period of adjustment and then the proverbial flipping of the switch. That pattern didn't quite play out in the majors. Rather, rare were the moments that Bichette did not look the part of a big-league star. He hit, he fielded and ran the bases with exactly the right kind of reckless abandon. His debut was a 200-plate appearance shot of adrenaline in a Blue Jays season needing precisely that. Concerns about his swing and/or approach were set aside so quickly that finding them will be tricky when they're needed (sometime in early-to-mid 2020, during his first prolonged slump).

The role of human espresso was supposed to be played by the Blue Jays' other gifted second-generation stud: Guerrero Jr. His rookie season did not go according to script, however, and he was not the Blue Jays' best player, the way most scouts and analysts proposed he would be before his early-season promotion. On a rate basis, that distinction instead went to Bichette. To be clear: Guerrero was okay—he was a league-average hitter who wowed crowds at the Home Run Derby and during his patented hot streaks; he just appeared more mortal than anticipated, struggling mightily in the field and hitting grounders too frequently.

Last season was the time for the Blue Jays to give these players space to learn, fail, thrive and become accustomed to the life of big-league ballplaying. (The college experience they missed out on, basically.) Last season was also the time for the organization to reinstill confidence in the fan base by demonstrating competence and showcasing the so-called future. It was probably more successful than intended.

⚾ ⚾ ⚾

Over the last few years, monarch numbers have upticked across the continent, countering a 20-year downward trend. The gains made are still far from re-establishing their numbers to where they were in the early 1990s, but it's a start.

Monarchs face considerable hardship in their continent-spanning migration, as factors such as habitat loss and climate change make an already arduous journey even more difficult. As numbers dipped over the last decade, grassroots efforts encouraged ordinary people along the migration route to plant milkweed (a larvae host plant for monarch butterflies) in their yards, gardens or—in the case of heavily urbanized areas such as the tangle of high-rise buildings surrounding the Blue Jays' ballpark—on their balconies.

World Wildlife Fund-Canada's senior species specialist Emily Giles noted that the Rogers Centre is on the monarch's migration path as it makes its way to Mexico, where they congregate around the start of November. "Monarchs need a lot of local nectar sources, as the journey south is quite taxing, physiologically speaking, and they feed on nectar which gives them high-energy fuel for the long journey."

⚾ ⚾ ⚾

Whereas monarchs move south around November, the Blue Jays are southern residents during the early portion of the year. Sleepy Dunedin has been their only exhibition-season home since 1977 and—after some politicking in 2016—will as such for at least another 20 years.

Overhauling their spring complex has become a major passion point for president and CEO Mark Shapiro. The Blue Jays now believe their spring facility will provide them with a competitive advantage that will help the club overcome the financial gap between them and their American League East rivals.

During a quiet moment before a media appearance, Shapiro thumbed through photos and explained the work being done ahead of the park's grand opening. "Development isn't something you do to players," Shapiro explained on a 2019 podcast appearance. "Our job is to give them the best resources—mentally, physically and fundamentally, as well as tools like buildings, equipment and technology—to help give them a plan, and then work with them to be the best they can be."

The tools and equipment that the Blue Jays believe will help rise tide that floats all boats include three "sports labs," two "fuel bars," a "movement studio" as well as plunge pools, saunas and more. It is here they'll eat and train together, collaborate, share information and toil joyfully in pursuit of personal fulfillment and free-agent dollars. They'll swap hitting tips and create TikToks, increasing camaraderie and launch angles in equal measure.

Shapiro and the Blue Jays organization believe it is here they plan to go from last to first, initially in terms of complex quality with on-field results lining up soon thereafter. Why spend money on good players when you can just grow your own, yanking cloned babies out of a high-tech river like Adrian Veidt?

⚾ ⚾ ⚾

The Blue Jays of the present and the future exist concurrently. Much of the prospect food is on the table, with Guerrero Jr. and Bichette representing the main course and established as everyday players. Top pitching prospect Nate Pearson is knocking on the door with dessert, too.

But the ongoing austerity efforts and firm insistence that spending and revenues remain "aligned" means the Blue Jays need their big-name, high-ceiling young talent to fulfill their promise—with the club using its expensive redone complex as a lazarus pit of sorts, wherein instructors dip various mid-round picks until one surfaces as a valued asset.

# Toronto Blue Jays 2020

Though the butterfly that landed on Britton's glove on the clear September night made for an unforgettable scene during an immensely forgettable baseball game, it wasn't likely to end well for the in-game field invader. Instead of being tackled by private security or ejected by an usher, any butterfly reaching the sickly green turf at the Rogers Centre was unlikely to ever taste the sweet nectar of freedom again, as WWF-Canada's Giles explains: "Once that individual butterfly made its way into the dome, it likely would've had trouble getting out as there's nothing but fake turf, pizza, and beer and no high-energy sources that a butterfly can readily use."

Getting good players to Toronto is one thing. Can the Blue Jays get them to become great players and, ideally, key parts of a great team? The test at this stage of the organization's trajectory is simple: grow something wonderful in a place historically hostile to the natural world.

*—Drew Fairservice is the co-host of the Birds All Day podcast.*

# Part 2: Player Analysis

# Toronto Blue Jays 2020

## PLAYER COMMENTS WITH GRAPHS

### Bo Bichette  SS
Born: 03/05/98  Age: 22  Bats: R  Throws: R
Height: 6'0"  Weight: 185  Origin: Round 2, 2016 Draft (#66 overall)

| YEAR | TEAM | LVL | AGE | PA  | R  | 2B | 3B | HR | RBI | BB | K   | SB | CS | AVG/OBP/SLG      |
|------|------|-----|-----|-----|----|----|----|----|-----|----|-----|----|----|------------------|
| 2017 | LNS  | A   | 19  | 317 | 60 | 32 | 3  | 10 | 51  | 28 | 55  | 12 | 3  | .384/.448/.623   |
| 2017 | DUN  | A+  | 19  | 182 | 28 | 9  | 1  | 4  | 23  | 14 | 26  | 10 | 4  | .323/.379/.463   |
| 2018 | NHP  | AA  | 20  | 595 | 95 | 43 | 7  | 11 | 74  | 48 | 101 | 32 | 11 | .286/.343/.453   |
| 2019 | BUF  | AAA | 21  | 244 | 34 | 16 | 2  | 8  | 32  | 19 | 48  | 15 | 5  | .275/.333/.473   |
| 2019 | TOR  | MLB | 21  | 212 | 32 | 18 | 0  | 11 | 21  | 14 | 50  | 4  | 4  | .311/.358/.571   |
| 2020 | TOR  | MLB | 22  | 595 | 68 | 33 | 3  | 23 | 78  | 40 | 137 | 15 | 6  | .260/.314/.454   |

Comparables: Orlando Arcia, Francisco Lindor, Wilmer Flores

As everyone expected, in 2019 the son of a major leaguer took the league by storm after debuting at a young age with serious hype (though an injury delayed his debut). The surprising part was that the player whose bat electrified was not Vladimir Guerrero, Jr. but Bichette. After debuting on July 29th, the former second-round pick dropped an OPS that was more than fifty points clear of any Jay with at least four trips to the plate on the season (Trent Thornton disclaimer alert). His DRC+ lagged though, mostly due to the randomness of hitting doubles—had Bichette continued his pace of two-baggers for a full season, he'd have finished with the most since 1936. The 22-year-old won't be eligible for Rookie of the Year considerations in 2020, but the combined potency of his bat and his glove at a key defensive position should warrant All-Star, and maybe even MVP, votes.

| YEAR | TEAM | LVL | AGE | PA  | DRC+ | VORP | BABIP | BRR  | FRAA                     | WARP |
|------|------|-----|-----|-----|------|------|-------|------|--------------------------|------|
| 2017 | LNS  | A   | 19  | 317 | 210  | 49.2 | .452  | 3.0  | SS(51): 0.2, 2B(14): 0.3 | 5.5  |
| 2017 | DUN  | A+  | 19  | 182 | 154  | 12.9 | .360  | -0.2 | SS(35): -0.3             | 1.5  |
| 2018 | NHP  | AA  | 20  | 595 | 127  | 40.6 | .331  | 3.2  | SS(116): -4.0, 2B(9): 0.6| 4.2  |
| 2019 | BUF  | AAA | 21  | 244 | 103  | 10.7 | .317  | -2.0 | SS(51): -1.4, 2B(1): 0.0 | 0.8  |
| 2019 | TOR  | MLB | 21  | 212 | 109  | 12.1 | .368  | -0.8 | SS(42): 4.6              | 1.5  |
| 2020 | TOR  | MLB | 22  | 595 | 101  | 23.2 | .308  | 0.1  | SS 2                     | 2.6  |

**Bo Bichette, continued**

### Batted Ball Distribution

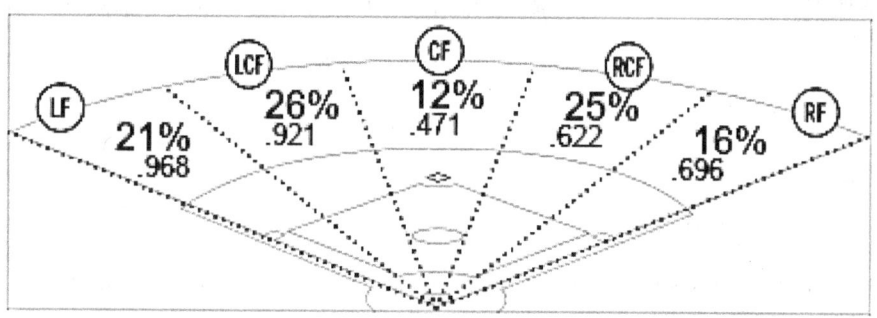

### Strike Zone vs LHP    Strike Zone vs RHP

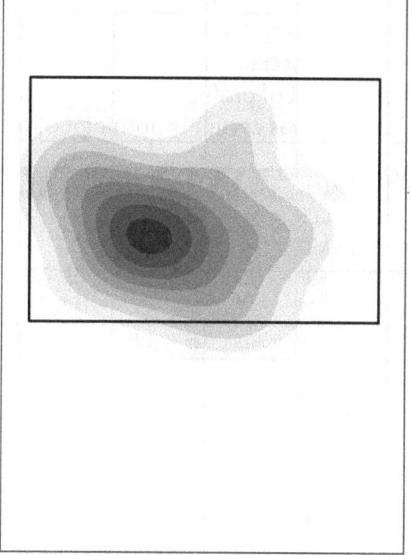

## Cavan Biggio  2B

Born: 04/11/95  Age: 25  Bats: L  Throws: R
Height: 6'2"  Weight: 200  Origin: Round 5, 2016 Draft (#162 overall)

| YEAR | TEAM | LVL | AGE | PA | R | 2B | 3B | HR | RBI | BB | K | SB | CS | AVG/OBP/SLG |
|---|---|---|---|---|---|---|---|---|---|---|---|---|---|---|
| 2017 | DUN | A+ | 22 | 556 | 75 | 17 | 5 | 11 | 60 | 74 | 140 | 11 | 7 | .233/.342/.363 |
| 2018 | NHP | AA | 23 | 563 | 80 | 23 | 5 | 26 | 99 | 100 | 148 | 20 | 8 | .252/.388/.499 |
| 2019 | BUF | AAA | 24 | 174 | 23 | 8 | 1 | 6 | 27 | 34 | 28 | 5 | 1 | .312/.448/.514 |
| 2019 | TOR | MLB | 24 | 430 | 66 | 17 | 2 | 16 | 48 | 71 | 123 | 14 | 0 | .234/.364/.429 |
| 2020 | TOR | MLB | 25 | 595 | 79 | 25 | 3 | 26 | 82 | 90 | 162 | 10 | 4 | .245/.365/.462 |

Comparables: Brandon Lowe, Nick Solak, Carlos Santana

You might get the sense Biggio is used to the shadows—a Hall of Fame dad, three teammates with better prospect cred whose fathers were also pros, a "next five" placement on the Blue Jays' 2019 prospect list. His first name comes from "the hollow" in Irish (*An Cabhán*), for goodness' sake. But if Biggio is acquainted with the shadows, he's surely used to carving out his own light, and got a start on that in a solid rookie season: his on-base percentage was the highest among his teammates with at least four plate appearances (Trent Thornton disclaimer alert), and he appears competent at second base. It's not the flashiest of profiles moving forward, but the same was true retrospectively, and there was certainly nothing hollow about his impressive 2019.

| YEAR | TEAM | LVL | AGE | PA | DRC+ | VORP | BABIP | BRR | FRAA | WARP |
|---|---|---|---|---|---|---|---|---|---|---|
| 2017 | DUN | A+ | 22 | 556 | 94 | 11.0 | .304 | 1.1 | 2B(116): 6.4, 3B(6): -0.4 | 2.1 |
| 2018 | NHP | AA | 23 | 563 | 137 | 44.8 | .307 | 3.6 | 2B(68): 1.5, 3B(34): -1.1 | 4.4 |
| 2019 | BUF | AAA | 24 | 174 | 150 | 19.7 | .352 | 0.5 | 2B(22): 2.0, 1B(7): 0.2 | 1.7 |
| 2019 | TOR | MLB | 24 | 430 | 112 | 20.5 | .309 | 2.2 | 2B(85): 0.5, RF(8): -0.9 | 2.1 |
| 2020 | TOR | MLB | 25 | 595 | 115 | 36.2 | .309 | 0.2 | 2B 4 | 4.1 |

*Cavan Biggio, continued*

**Batted Ball Distribution**

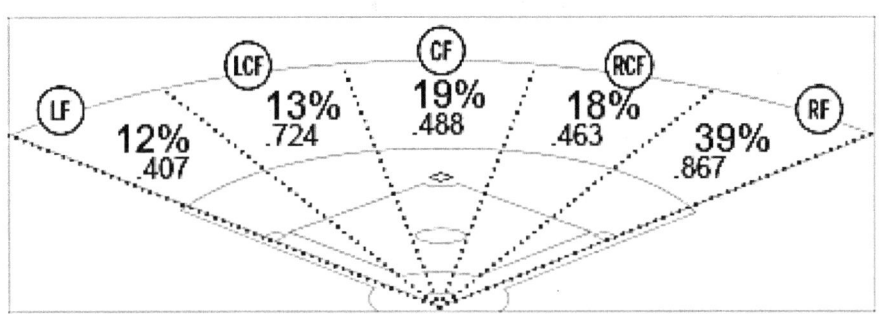

**Strike Zone vs LHP**  **Strike Zone vs RHP**

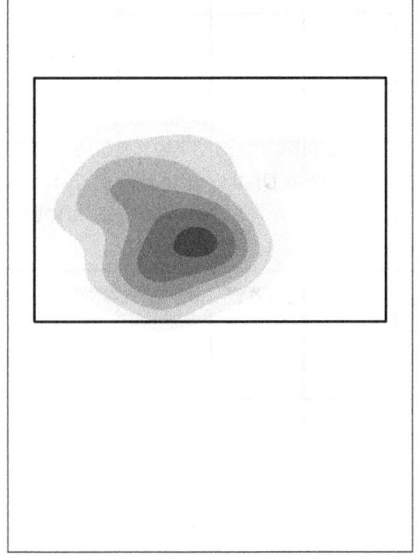

Toronto Blue Jays 2020

## Brandon Drury 3B

Born: 08/21/92  Age: 27  Bats: R  Throws: R
Height: 6'2"  Weight: 215  Origin: Round 13, 2010 Draft (#404 overall)

| YEAR | TEAM | LVL | AGE | PA | R | 2B | 3B | HR | RBI | BB | K | SB | CS | AVG/OBP/SLG |
|---|---|---|---|---|---|---|---|---|---|---|---|---|---|---|
| 2017 | ARI | MLB | 24 | 480 | 41 | 37 | 2 | 13 | 63 | 28 | 103 | 1 | 1 | .267/.317/.447 |
| 2018 | TRN | AA | 25 | 25 | 4 | 0 | 0 | 1 | 2 | 5 | 10 | 0 | 0 | .263/.400/.421 |
| 2018 | SWB | AAA | 25 | 235 | 30 | 13 | 1 | 5 | 30 | 32 | 58 | 3 | 1 | .291/.400/.442 |
| 2018 | NYA | MLB | 25 | 57 | 2 | 2 | 0 | 1 | 7 | 5 | 12 | 0 | 0 | .176/.263/.275 |
| 2018 | TOR | MLB | 25 | 29 | 3 | 2 | 0 | 0 | 3 | 2 | 8 | 0 | 0 | .154/.241/.231 |
| 2019 | TOR | MLB | 26 | 447 | 43 | 21 | 1 | 15 | 41 | 25 | 113 | 0 | 1 | .218/.262/.380 |
| 2020 | TOR | MLB | 27 | 280 | 29 | 16 | 1 | 9 | 34 | 18 | 67 | 1 | 1 | .235/.290/.408 |

Comparables: Manny Machado, Aramis Ramirez, Jim Presley

Drury Lane is the protagonist of a quartet of 1930s detective novels published via a pseudonym-inside-a-synonym; in the books a retired actor quotes Hamlet and solves the cases no one else can, before in the fourth novel meeting a fittingly Shakespearean end. Now there's a mystery afoot in Toronto, namely how long they can sustain this sort of performance from their own Drury. It's no Hamlet, but it's been properly Shakespearean in tragedy. Forced into everyday play for much of the season due to pervasive injuries on the team, Drury was just abysmal with the bat (even by his standards) and squarely below-average in the field. Moving into his second of four swings at arbitration (it's probably for the best that Drury, who ran a 25-percent strikeout rate last year, gets an extra cut), one wonders if he will get another chance to make good on the J.A. Happ trade.

| YEAR | TEAM | LVL | AGE | PA | DRC+ | VORP | BABIP | BRR | FRAA | WARP |
|---|---|---|---|---|---|---|---|---|---|---|
| 2017 | ARI | MLB | 24 | 480 | 83 | 9.8 | .320 | -3.9 | 2B(114): 2.5, 3B(1): -0.2 | 0.3 |
| 2018 | TRN | AA | 25 | 25 | 109 | 3.3 | .444 | 0.2 | 3B(4): -0.2 | 0.1 |
| 2018 | SWB | AAA | 25 | 235 | 134 | 19.7 | .390 | -1.0 | 3B(45): 2.4, 1B(5): 0.7 | 1.7 |
| 2018 | NYA | MLB | 25 | 57 | 78 | -2.1 | .211 | 0.1 | 3B(9): -0.7, 2B(5): -0.1 | -0.1 |
| 2018 | TOR | MLB | 25 | 29 | 80 | -1.8 | .222 | 0.0 | 3B(6): -0.1, 2B(2): -0.6 | 0.0 |
| 2019 | TOR | MLB | 26 | 447 | 70 | -2.6 | .259 | 0.4 | 3B(65): -1.2, RF(18): -2.1 | -0.7 |
| 2020 | TOR | MLB | 27 | 280 | 81 | -0.5 | .281 | -0.7 | 1B -3, 2B 0 | -0.3 |

**Brandon Drury, continued**

### Batted Ball Distribution

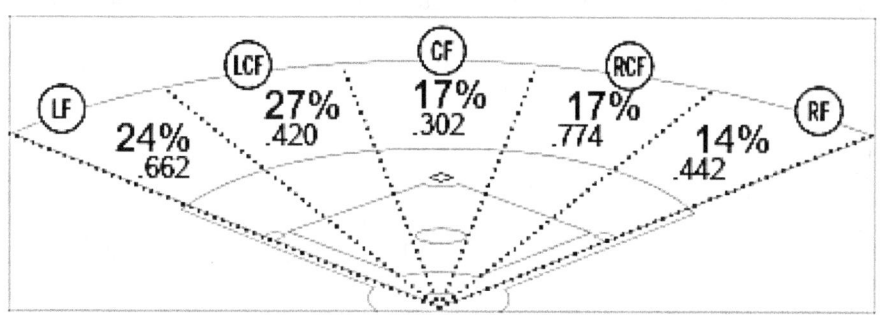

### Strike Zone vs LHP

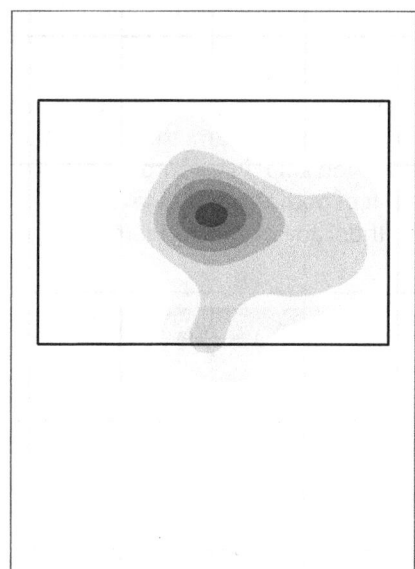

### Strike Zone vs RHP

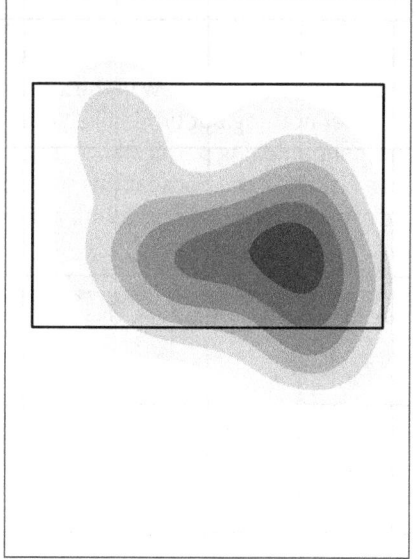

# Toronto Blue Jays 2020

## Derek Fisher  OF
Born: 08/21/93   Age: 26   Bats: L   Throws: R
Height: 6'3"   Weight: 205   Origin: Round 1, 2014 Draft (#37 overall)

| YEAR | TEAM | LVL | AGE | PA | R | 2B | 3B | HR | RBI | BB | K | SB | CS | AVG/OBP/SLG |
|---|---|---|---|---|---|---|---|---|---|---|---|---|---|---|
| 2017 | FRE | AAA | 23 | 384 | 63 | 26 | 1 | 21 | 66 | 35 | 74 | 16 | 10 | .318/.384/.583 |
| 2017 | HOU | MLB | 23 | 166 | 21 | 4 | 1 | 5 | 17 | 17 | 54 | 3 | 3 | .212/.307/.356 |
| 2018 | FRE | AAA | 24 | 281 | 44 | 12 | 1 | 10 | 34 | 39 | 85 | 11 | 1 | .251/.363/.435 |
| 2018 | HOU | MLB | 24 | 86 | 13 | 2 | 2 | 4 | 11 | 5 | 42 | 2 | 0 | .165/.209/.392 |
| 2019 | ROU | AAA | 25 | 270 | 44 | 9 | 1 | 14 | 36 | 40 | 67 | 8 | 3 | .286/.401/.522 |
| 2019 | TOR | MLB | 25 | 107 | 14 | 2 | 0 | 6 | 12 | 14 | 43 | 1 | 0 | .161/.271/.376 |
| 2019 | HOU | MLB | 25 | 60 | 9 | 2 | 1 | 1 | 5 | 7 | 14 | 4 | 1 | .226/.317/.358 |
| 2020 | TOR | MLB | 26 | 315 | 42 | 12 | 1 | 17 | 47 | 36 | 107 | 9 | 3 | .235/.328/.477 |

Comparables: Kirk Nieuwenhuis, Brett Jackson, Matt Joyce

Long a bundle of kinetic energy ready to actualize, Fisher has just needed to get in motion. He ran out of time to do so, however, in Houston—regardless of his fourth consecutive year punishing the PCL—Fisher was unable to break into a defined role. With the blocks in front of his path concretizing, the Astros netted Aaron Sanchez, Joe Biagini, and prospect Cal Stevenson for the glimmer of possibility teams still saw in the 2014 first round pick. Conversely, the Blue Jays can offer nothing but time—likely something to do with the metric system. Still, another punishing performance (but not the good kind) in his Toronto debut will have Fisher on the hot seat this season, bereft of both minor league options and the expectations that come with nearly a half-decade of gracing team prospect lists.

| YEAR | TEAM | LVL | AGE | PA | DRC+ | VORP | BABIP | BRR | FRAA | WARP |
|---|---|---|---|---|---|---|---|---|---|---|
| 2017 | FRE | AAA | 23 | 384 | 145 | 33.9 | .352 | -0.8 | CF(53): -5.3, LF(17): 2.3 | 2.9 |
| 2017 | HOU | MLB | 23 | 166 | 70 | -1.2 | .299 | -0.5 | LF(38): 1.2, RF(12): 0.0 | -0.1 |
| 2018 | FRE | AAA | 24 | 281 | 114 | 16.5 | .347 | 2.2 | CF(33): -2.7, LF(19): -0.7 | 1.1 |
| 2018 | HOU | MLB | 24 | 86 | 48 | 1.6 | .257 | 1.6 | LF(26): -1.3, CF(9): -0.4 | -0.3 |
| 2019 | ROU | AAA | 25 | 270 | 122 | 24.3 | .347 | -0.5 | CF(29): 1.5, RF(21): 1.5 | 1.7 |
| 2019 | TOR | MLB | 25 | 107 | 67 | -1.5 | .205 | -0.4 | LF(27): 0.9, RF(4): -0.3 | -0.1 |
| 2019 | HOU | MLB | 25 | 60 | 83 | 0.2 | .289 | 1.0 | LF(11): 0.0, RF(5): 0.4 | 0.1 |
| 2020 | TOR | MLB | 26 | 315 | 106 | 11.4 | .312 | 0.8 | RF 0, CF -1 | 1.1 |

**Derek Fisher, continued**

## Batted Ball Distribution

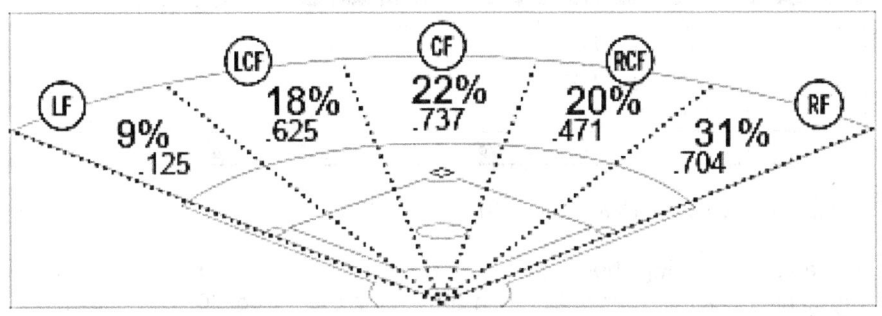

## Strike Zone vs LHP    Strike Zone vs RHP

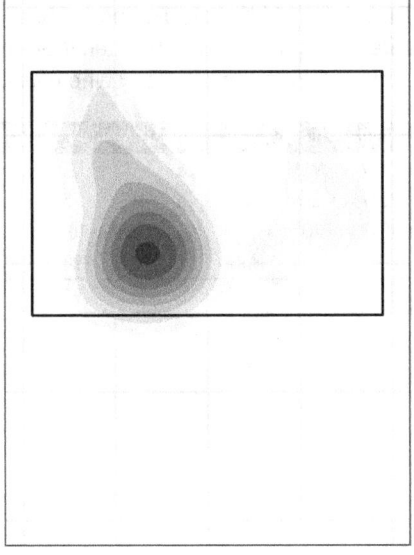

## Randal Grichuk  RF

Born: 08/13/91  Age: 28  Bats: R  Throws: R
Height: 6'2"  Weight: 213  Origin: Round 1, 2009 Draft (#24 overall)

| YEAR | TEAM | LVL | AGE | PA | R | 2B | 3B | HR | RBI | BB | K | SB | CS | AVG/OBP/SLG |
|------|------|-----|-----|-----|----|----|----|----|-----|----|-----|----|----|--------------|
| 2017 | MEM | AAA | 25 | 67 | 11 | 3 | 0 | 6 | 9 | 3 | 20 | 0 | 0 | .270/.313/.603 |
| 2017 | SLN | MLB | 25 | 442 | 53 | 25 | 3 | 22 | 59 | 26 | 133 | 6 | 1 | .238/.285/.473 |
| 2018 | TOR | MLB | 26 | 462 | 60 | 32 | 1 | 25 | 61 | 27 | 122 | 3 | 2 | .245/.301/.502 |
| 2019 | TOR | MLB | 27 | 628 | 75 | 29 | 5 | 31 | 80 | 35 | 163 | 2 | 1 | .232/.280/.457 |
| 2020 | TOR | MLB | 28 | 595 | 72 | 28 | 4 | 33 | 91 | 35 | 167 | 6 | 2 | .230/.282/.475 |

Comparables: Jay Bruce, Wil Myers, Jorge Soler

We can say one thing about Grichuk for certain: he is going to be around. With the signing of a five-year, $52 million contract at the start of 2019, Grichuk has security in spite of a season that otherwise would have seen him a likely DFA candidate. Like everyone else in 2019, the 28-year-old hit 31 home runs, but his OBP finally hit rock bottom and while his strikeout-to-walk rate would be elite for a pitcher, Grichuk does not pitch. Four years remain on the pact between the Blue Jays and their too-often center fielder (any amount of him there is too often), so it remains to be seen if Grichuk spends them as "guy on a bad contract" or reverts to "guy who was picked directly in front of Mike Trout."

| YEAR | TEAM | LVL | AGE | PA | DRC+ | VORP | BABIP | BRR | FRAA | WARP |
|------|------|-----|-----|-----|------|------|-------|------|------|------|
| 2017 | MEM | AAA | 25 | 67 | 123 | 5.0 | .297 | 0.0 | LF(9): 3.6, CF(1): -0.1 | 0.7 |
| 2017 | SLN | MLB | 25 | 442 | 95 | 11.9 | .293 | 1.9 | LF(58): -2.7, RF(55): 4.8 | 1.2 |
| 2018 | TOR | MLB | 26 | 462 | 109 | 19.0 | .282 | 2.5 | RF(102): 2.4, CF(26): -2.3 | 1.9 |
| 2019 | TOR | MLB | 27 | 628 | 90 | 9.7 | .266 | -0.2 | RF(92): -3.2, CF(62): -4.9 | 0.1 |
| 2020 | TOR | MLB | 28 | 595 | 91 | 11.8 | .266 | 1.2 | RF 1, CF -7 | 0.6 |

*Randal Grichuk, continued*

**Batted Ball Distribution**

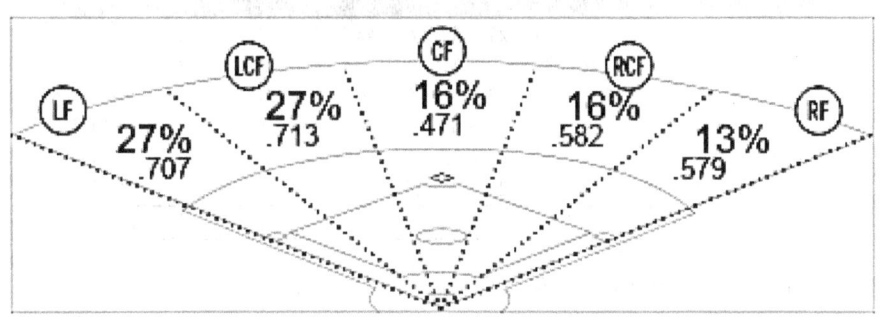

**Strike Zone vs LHP**  **Strike Zone vs RHP**

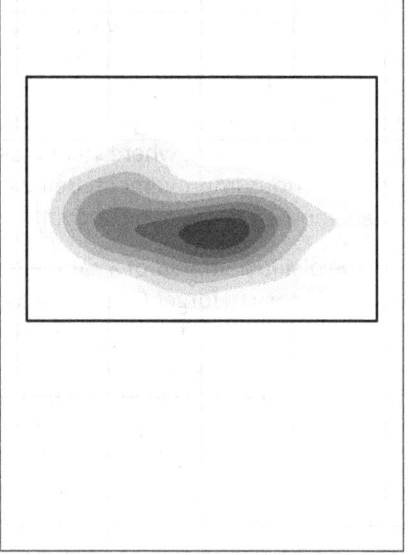

## Toronto Blue Jays 2020

### Vladimir Guerrero Jr.  3B

Born: 03/16/99   Age: 21   Bats: R   Throws: R
Height: 6'2"   Weight: 250   Origin: International Free Agent, 2015

| YEAR | TEAM | LVL | AGE | PA | R | 2B | 3B | HR | RBI | BB | K | SB | CS | AVG/OBP/SLG |
|---|---|---|---|---|---|---|---|---|---|---|---|---|---|---|
| 2017 | LNS | A | 18 | 318 | 53 | 21 | 1 | 7 | 45 | 40 | 34 | 6 | 2 | .316/.409/.480 |
| 2017 | DUN | A+ | 18 | 209 | 31 | 7 | 1 | 6 | 31 | 36 | 28 | 2 | 2 | .333/.450/.494 |
| 2018 | NHP | AA | 19 | 266 | 48 | 19 | 1 | 14 | 60 | 21 | 27 | 3 | 3 | .402/.449/.671 |
| 2018 | BUF | AAA | 19 | 128 | 15 | 7 | 0 | 6 | 16 | 15 | 10 | 0 | 0 | .336/.414/.564 |
| 2019 | BUF | AAA | 20 | 34 | 7 | 1 | 0 | 3 | 8 | 4 | 2 | 1 | 0 | .367/.441/.700 |
| 2019 | TOR | MLB | 20 | 514 | 52 | 26 | 2 | 15 | 69 | 46 | 91 | 0 | 1 | .272/.339/.433 |
| 2020 | TOR | MLB | 21 | 630 | 77 | 33 | 2 | 26 | 87 | 53 | 105 | 4 | 2 | .273/.339/.473 |

Comparables: Carlos Correa, Ronald Acuña Jr., Ozzie Albies

Guerrero is the Prince That Was Promised, the one prophesied to fight the darkness and save the North. If you watched *Game of Thrones*, you probably know that didn't amount to all that much, and you'd be forgiven for feeling similarly about the debut season of the most hyped prospect of the last half of the 2010s. The 20-year-old wasn't bad by any means, but with a batting line that rated as basically average, he was neither the best rookie in the league nor on his own team. After the year-long waiting game of the Jays' service time manipulation, the landing was decidedly underwhelming. The defense was bad-to-untenable at third, where Vladito likely won't stick even 'til arbitration without serious improvement. Being one of the 25 worst runners in the league added another vector of disappointment.

In the disillusionment of a campaign that ultimately amounted to an average player, it's easy to forget Guerrero was just 20 years old, a year beyond the legal drinking age in Toronto but massively outstripping the huge majority of the league in his speed of development. It was the first chapter of a book that has yet to be written, and while it might not have immediately drawn in the readers, not every book must—especially when, as with Guerrero, a foundation is being built. He might still be the Prince That Was Promised, but rather than the *Game of Thrones*' version he will have to be the model from *A Song of Ice and Fire*. Like George R.R. Martin's series, the rest is not yet written. Even after seeing what we have on screen, audiences can immerse ourselves in the limitless possibility of Guerrero's potential, the dream that everything will be put to right when a new chapter is inked.

| YEAR | TEAM | LVL | AGE | PA | DRC+ | VORP | BABIP | BRR | FRAA | WARP |
|---|---|---|---|---|---|---|---|---|---|---|
| 2017 | LNS | A | 18 | 318 | 172 | 27.5 | .336 | 0.8 | 3B(61): -2.6 | 3.3 |
| 2017 | DUN | A+ | 18 | 209 | 196 | 17.7 | .365 | -2.4 | 3B(41): -1.5 | 2.0 |
| 2018 | NHP | AA | 19 | 266 | 196 | 37.4 | .402 | -2.9 | 3B(53): 1.0 | 3.3 |
| 2018 | BUF | AAA | 19 | 128 | 194 | 11.5 | .323 | -4.8 | 3B(25): 4.3 | 1.5 |
| 2019 | BUF | AAA | 20 | 34 | 159 | 5.5 | .320 | -0.2 | 3B(7): 0.1 | 0.3 |
| 2019 | TOR | MLB | 20 | 514 | 101 | 18.0 | .308 | -3.5 | 3B(96): -5.1 | 0.9 |
| 2020 | TOR | MLB | 21 | 630 | 113 | 21.7 | .295 | -2.4 | 3B 0 | 2.3 |

*Vladimir Guerrero Jr., continued*

**Batted Ball Distribution**

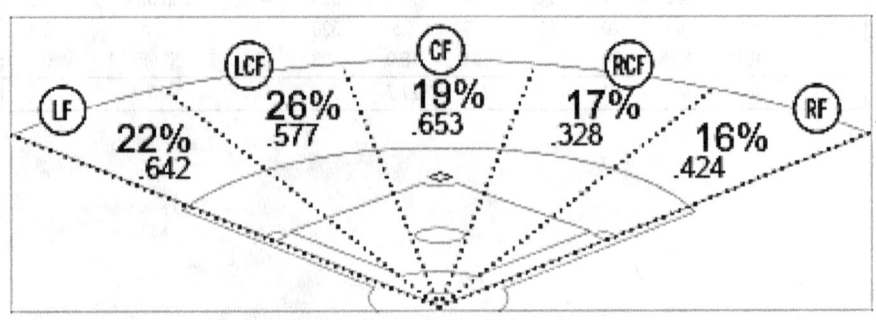

**Strike Zone vs LHP**   **Strike Zone vs RHP**

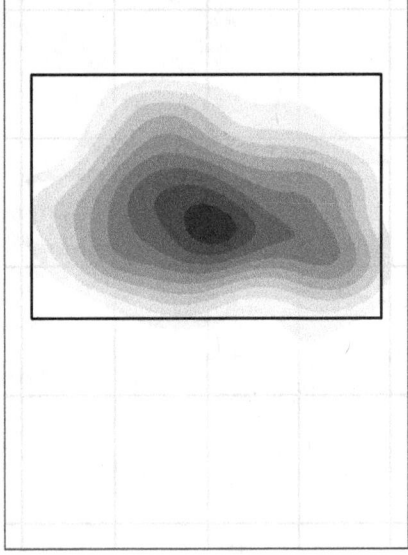

## Lourdes Gurriel Jr.  LF

Born: 10/10/93  Age: 26  Bats: R  Throws: R
Height: 6'3"  Weight: 215  Origin: International Free Agent, 2016

| YEAR | TEAM | LVL | AGE | PA | R | 2B | 3B | HR | RBI | BB | K | SB | CS | AVG/OBP/SLG |
|---|---|---|---|---|---|---|---|---|---|---|---|---|---|---|
| 2017 | DUN | A+ | 23 | 69 | 6 | 1 | 0 | 1 | 8 | 2 | 13 | 1 | 0 | .197/.217/.258 |
| 2017 | NHP | AA | 23 | 185 | 20 | 10 | 0 | 4 | 28 | 10 | 30 | 2 | 0 | .241/.286/.371 |
| 2018 | NHP | AA | 24 | 65 | 7 | 3 | 1 | 2 | 14 | 3 | 8 | 1 | 1 | .322/.354/.508 |
| 2018 | BUF | AAA | 24 | 156 | 20 | 8 | 0 | 5 | 30 | 4 | 34 | 3 | 2 | .293/.321/.449 |
| 2018 | TOR | MLB | 24 | 263 | 30 | 8 | 0 | 11 | 35 | 9 | 59 | 1 | 2 | .281/.309/.446 |
| 2019 | BUF | AAA | 25 | 130 | 18 | 13 | 0 | 4 | 26 | 3 | 23 | 0 | 2 | .276/.308/.480 |
| 2019 | TOR | MLB | 25 | 343 | 52 | 19 | 2 | 20 | 50 | 20 | 86 | 6 | 4 | .277/.327/.541 |
| 2020 | TOR | MLB | 26 | 595 | 70 | 30 | 1 | 29 | 85 | 26 | 141 | 4 | 2 | .251/.293/.463 |

Comparables: Troy Tulowitzki, José Rondón, Charlie Culberson

Son of a renowned ballplayer, the best hitter on the Blue Jays by DRC+: sorry, did you think this was someone other than Gurriel Jr.? While an imprecise arm at the keystone earned him an early-season demotion to figure out a new position and injuries kept the sophomore out for most of August and September, he improved at the plate in year two. The now left fielder (and not a bad one at that!) improved his walk rate and isolated power by more than 50 percent over his rookie campaign and even spiked his fly-ball rate by 10 percentage points on his way to 20 dingers. Hopefully in one of the four years remaining of Gurriel Jr.'s seven with the Jays, he will do more than flash tantalizing potential in brief stints. He'll be hard-pressed to best brother (and simultaneous Cuban defector) Yuli's career-high 31 homers from last season without a full campaign.

| YEAR | TEAM | LVL | AGE | PA | DRC+ | VORP | BABIP | BRR | FRAA | WARP |
|---|---|---|---|---|---|---|---|---|---|---|
| 2017 | DUN | A+ | 23 | 69 | 57 | -3.2 | .226 | 0.3 | SS(11): -0.2, 2B(1): 0.1 | 0.0 |
| 2017 | NHP | AA | 23 | 185 | 73 | 4.0 | .266 | 1.2 | 2B(22): 1.5, SS(17): 0.9 | 0.5 |
| 2018 | NHP | AA | 24 | 65 | 129 | 6.7 | .333 | 0.3 | 2B(7): -0.1, SS(5): -0.7 | 0.4 |
| 2018 | BUF | AAA | 24 | 156 | 118 | 7.0 | .345 | -0.9 | SS(23): 0.9, 2B(9): 0.2 | 0.9 |
| 2018 | TOR | MLB | 24 | 263 | 104 | 8.8 | .326 | -1.7 | SS(46): -0.8, 2B(24): -1.1 | 0.8 |
| 2019 | BUF | AAA | 25 | 130 | 104 | 1.5 | .309 | -3.6 | 2B(12): -1.1, SS(7): -2.0 | -0.2 |
| 2019 | TOR | MLB | 25 | 343 | 113 | 14.9 | .318 | 2.0 | LF(63): -0.1, 2B(9): -1.3 | 1.5 |
| 2020 | TOR | MLB | 26 | 595 | 96 | 11.5 | .285 | 0.8 | LF -10 | 0.2 |

*Lourdes Gurriel Jr., continued*

**Batted Ball Distribution**

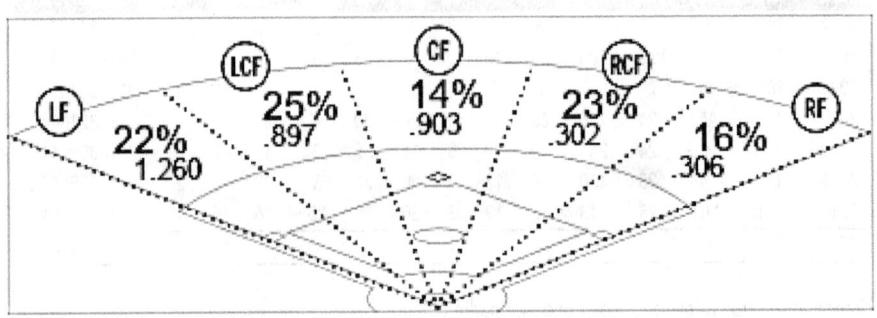

**Strike Zone vs LHP**  **Strike Zone vs RHP**

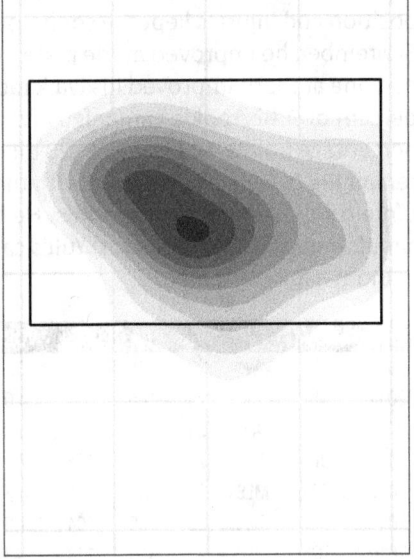

## Teoscar Hernández  OF

Born: 10/15/92  Age: 27  Bats: R  Throws: R
Height: 6'2"  Weight: 205  Origin: International Free Agent, 2011

| YEAR | TEAM | LVL | AGE | PA | R | 2B | 3B | HR | RBI | BB | K | SB | CS | AVG/OBP/SLG |
|---|---|---|---|---|---|---|---|---|---|---|---|---|---|---|
| 2017 | FRE | AAA | 24 | 347 | 54 | 20 | 3 | 12 | 44 | 39 | 72 | 12 | 7 | .279/.369/.485 |
| 2017 | BUF | AAA | 24 | 109 | 14 | 6 | 2 | 6 | 22 | 8 | 30 | 4 | 1 | .222/.294/.505 |
| 2017 | TOR | MLB | 24 | 95 | 16 | 6 | 0 | 8 | 20 | 6 | 36 | 0 | 1 | .261/.305/.602 |
| 2018 | TOR | MLB | 25 | 523 | 67 | 29 | 7 | 22 | 57 | 41 | 163 | 5 | 5 | .239/.302/.468 |
| 2019 | BUF | AAA | 26 | 83 | 11 | 0 | 1 | 5 | 11 | 6 | 21 | 3 | 0 | .253/.313/.480 |
| 2019 | TOR | MLB | 26 | 464 | 58 | 19 | 2 | 26 | 65 | 45 | 153 | 6 | 3 | .230/.306/.472 |
| 2020 | TOR | MLB | 27 | 595 | 77 | 27 | 3 | 33 | 91 | 49 | 191 | 16 | 7 | .235/.303/.481 |

Comparables: Pete Incaviglia, Melvin Nieves, Aaron Cunningham

Hernández has long been a player around whom evaluators saw an uncertain future: not a solid enough defender to play center, unclear if the bat would support him as an everyday corner outfielder. The forecast only grew gloomier as Hernández distinguished himself with the glove in a negative sense in his first full campaign and showed only a league-average bat. This year the glove was markedly improved, but an extended slump to start the season led to a demotion to Buffalo. Upon his return Hernández put up an .873 OPS the rest of the way, and suddenly there's reason to think everything has come together for him—long something of a Magic Eye painting, the Blue Jays have finally stayed still long enough for them to see cohesion among mess.

| YEAR | TEAM | LVL | AGE | PA | DRC+ | VORP | BABIP | BRR | FRAA | WARP |
|---|---|---|---|---|---|---|---|---|---|---|
| 2017 | FRE | AAA | 24 | 347 | 122 | 22.7 | .329 | 1.9 | RF(44): 2.2, CF(22): 1.4 | 2.3 |
| 2017 | BUF | AAA | 24 | 109 | 99 | 4.9 | .254 | 0.8 | RF(10): 0.8, CF(7): 1.0 | 0.9 |
| 2017 | TOR | MLB | 24 | 95 | 101 | 8.5 | .333 | 1.9 | LF(18): -0.7, CF(5): 0.0 | 0.4 |
| 2018 | TOR | MLB | 25 | 523 | 104 | 12.4 | .313 | -0.1 | LF(87): -2.0, RF(35): 0.7 | 1.3 |
| 2019 | BUF | AAA | 26 | 83 | 84 | 3.3 | .280 | 0.8 | CF(9): -1.5, LF(5): 0.3 | 0.0 |
| 2019 | TOR | MLB | 26 | 464 | 100 | 16.0 | .293 | -0.4 | CF(79): -0.8, LF(46): 9.6 | 2.4 |
| 2020 | TOR | MLB | 27 | 595 | 101 | 16.6 | .296 | 0.8 | CF 4, LF 0 | 2.1 |

*Teoscar Hernández, continued*

**Batted Ball Distribution**

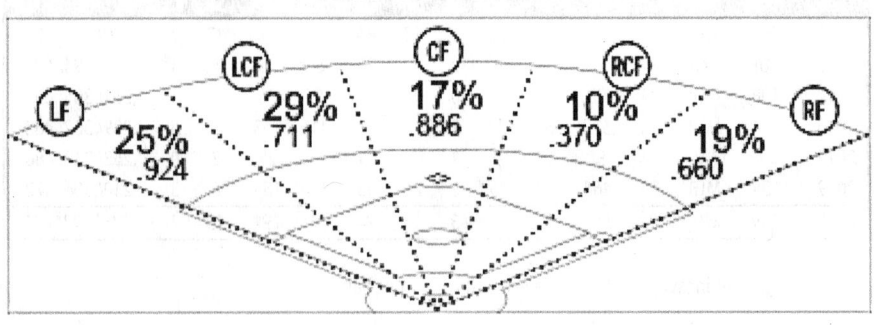

**Strike Zone vs LHP**     **Strike Zone vs RHP**

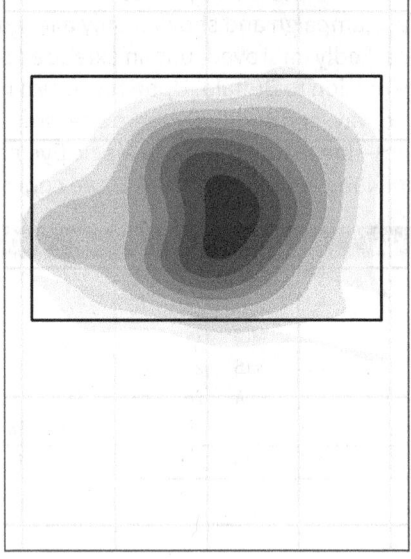

## Danny Jansen   C

Born: 04/15/95   Age: 25   Bats: R   Throws: R
Height: 6'2"   Weight: 230   Origin: Round 16, 2013 Draft (#475 overall)

| YEAR | TEAM | LVL | AGE | PA | R | 2B | 3B | HR | RBI | BB | K | SB | CS | AVG/OBP/SLG |
|---|---|---|---|---|---|---|---|---|---|---|---|---|---|---|
| 2017 | DUN | A+ | 22 | 136 | 19 | 6 | 0 | 5 | 18 | 8 | 14 | 0 | 0 | .369/.422/.541 |
| 2017 | NHP | AA | 22 | 210 | 23 | 15 | 1 | 2 | 20 | 22 | 19 | 1 | 0 | .291/.378/.419 |
| 2017 | BUF | AAA | 22 | 78 | 8 | 4 | 1 | 3 | 10 | 11 | 7 | 0 | 0 | .328/.423/.552 |
| 2018 | BUF | AAA | 23 | 360 | 45 | 21 | 1 | 12 | 58 | 44 | 49 | 5 | 1 | .275/.390/.473 |
| 2018 | TOR | MLB | 23 | 95 | 12 | 6 | 0 | 3 | 8 | 9 | 17 | 0 | 0 | .247/.347/.432 |
| 2019 | TOR | MLB | 24 | 384 | 41 | 12 | 1 | 13 | 43 | 31 | 79 | 0 | 1 | .207/.279/.360 |
| 2020 | TOR | MLB | 25 | 280 | 32 | 13 | 0 | 11 | 36 | 25 | 56 | 1 | 0 | .232/.313/.421 |

Comparables: Jim Pagliaroni, Chris Snyder, Max Kepler

Jansen's calling card was supposed to be the bat—not that he was considered a slouch from a defensive standpoint. His precipitous climb up the Toronto organizational rankings was sparked by a 2017 breakout season at the plate for which vision correction was credited. Yet, in a season where Jansen finally got his extended shot, it wasn't his work standing next to home plate but rather behind it that solidified him in the Blue Jays' plans for years to come. In fact, not only did Jansen finish sixth in the majors in CSAA, but the rookie was a finalist for a Gold Glove. He also made headlines in July for shaving his mustache mid-game after beginning the day hitless in three at-bats and then knocking in two during his next plate appearance. With a bat that grades as even average Jansen will be a top-10 catcher. Maybe it's just a matter of finding the right superstition.

| YEAR | TEAM | P. COUNT | FRM RUNS | BLK RUNS | THRW RUNS | TOT RUNS |
|---|---|---|---|---|---|---|
| 2017 | BUF | 2610 | 0.0 | 0.1 | -0.1 | 0.2 |
| 2017 | NHP | 6546 | -2.1 | 2.2 | 0.0 | -0.8 |
| 2018 | BUF | 7393 | -4.6 | 0.2 | -0.1 | -4.0 |
| 2018 | TOR | 3560 | 0.6 | 0.7 | -0.2 | 1.8 |
| 2019 | TOR | 14774 | 10.9 | 2.1 | 0.4 | 13.4 |
| 2020 | TOR | 10982 | 6.1 | 0.8 | 0.4 | 7.3 |

| YEAR | TEAM | LVL | AGE | PA | DRC+ | VORP | BABIP | BRR | FRAA | WARP |
|---|---|---|---|---|---|---|---|---|---|---|
| 2017 | DUN | A+ | 22 | 136 | 197 | 17.6 | .385 | -0.7 | C(25): -2.0 | 1.4 |
| 2017 | NHP | AA | 22 | 210 | 120 | 15.2 | .311 | -1.4 | C(52): -0.9 | 1.2 |
| 2017 | BUF | AAA | 22 | 78 | 170 | 11.2 | .333 | -0.1 | C(21): -0.4 | 0.8 |
| 2018 | BUF | AAA | 23 | 360 | 141 | 32.9 | .292 | 0.2 | C(56): -6.0 | 2.1 |
| 2018 | TOR | MLB | 23 | 95 | 100 | 6.5 | .274 | 0.9 | C(29): 1.0 | 0.7 |
| 2019 | TOR | MLB | 24 | 384 | 82 | 10.9 | .230 | -0.7 | C(103): 11.9 | 2.2 |
| 2020 | TOR | MLB | 25 | 280 | 94 | 11.1 | .256 | 0.2 | C 7 | 1.8 |

# Toronto Blue Jays 2020

*Danny Jansen, continued*

**Batted Ball Distribution**

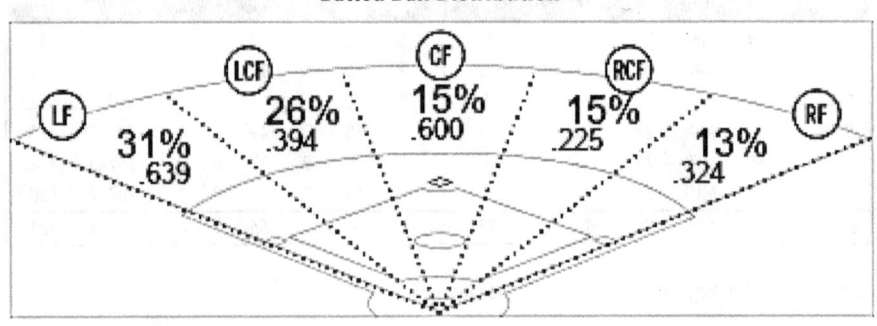

**Strike Zone vs LHP**   **Strike Zone vs RHP**

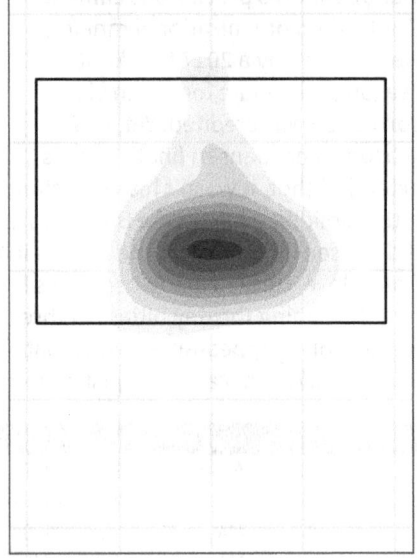

## Reese McGuire   C

Born: 03/02/95   Age: 25   Bats: L   Throws: R
Height: 6'0"   Weight: 215   Origin: Round 1, 2013 Draft (#14 overall)

| YEAR | TEAM | LVL | AGE | PA | R | 2B | 3B | HR | RBI | BB | K | SB | CS | AVG/OBP/SLG |
|---|---|---|---|---|---|---|---|---|---|---|---|---|---|---|
| 2017 | BLJ | RK | 22 | 26 | 4 | 2 | 0 | 0 | 7 | 3 | 1 | 0 | 1 | .409/.462/.500 |
| 2017 | NHP | AA | 22 | 136 | 19 | 5 | 1 | 6 | 20 | 16 | 19 | 2 | 1 | .278/.366/.496 |
| 2018 | BUF | AAA | 23 | 369 | 31 | 9 | 2 | 7 | 37 | 33 | 77 | 3 | 2 | .233/.312/.339 |
| 2018 | TOR | MLB | 23 | 33 | 5 | 3 | 0 | 2 | 4 | 2 | 9 | 1 | 0 | .290/.333/.581 |
| 2019 | BUF | AAA | 24 | 277 | 30 | 12 | 1 | 5 | 29 | 25 | 44 | 4 | 0 | .247/.316/.366 |
| 2019 | TOR | MLB | 24 | 105 | 14 | 7 | 0 | 5 | 11 | 7 | 18 | 0 | 0 | .299/.346/.526 |
| 2020 | TOR | MLB | 25 | 385 | 40 | 18 | 1 | 12 | 45 | 29 | 69 | 4 | 2 | .241/.304/.400 |

Comparables: Chance Sisco, L.J. Hoes, Tucker Barnhart

| YEAR | TEAM | P. COUNT | FRM RUNS | BLK RUNS | THRW RUNS | TOT RUNS |
|---|---|---|---|---|---|---|
| 2017 | NHP | 4206 | 4.4 | 0.1 | 0.0 | 4.6 |
| 2018 | BUF | 9552 | 15.4 | 0.2 | 0.3 | 15.9 |
| 2018 | TOR | 1355 | 0.4 | 0.5 | -0.1 | 1.0 |
| 2019 | BUF | 10029 | 7.0 | 0.0 | -1.5 | 5.8 |
| 2019 | TOR | 4094 | 5.0 | 0.4 | 0.0 | 5.7 |
| 2020 | TOR | 14758 | 13.8 | 1.2 | -0.7 | 14.3 |

In an episode of the Disney Channel series *Lizzie McGuire*, Hilary Duff's titular character fears her athletic prowess will prevent boys from taking an interest in her, and that her skills are having her misrepresented. While this McGuire need not be concerned about his strong performance with the bat in two brief stints turning off teams, that he has a .539 slugging percentage through his first 44 career games is likely a sizable misrepresentation of a player who had otherwise never surpassed .500 in his various minor league stints. Still, he need not fret about teams perceiving him incorrectly: at the end of the TV episode, Lizzie learns that she should just be herself and not worry about what others think. Given his defensive chops, the Jays backstop could take the same lesson—whether this level of offensive performance in MLB is sustainable, McGuire has what it takes to stick in a sizable role.

| YEAR | TEAM | LVL | AGE | PA | DRC+ | VORP | BABIP | BRR | FRAA | WARP |
|---|---|---|---|---|---|---|---|---|---|---|
| 2017 | BLJ | RK | 22 | 26 | 191 | 3.3 | .409 | -0.3 | C(4): 0.0 | 0.2 |
| 2017 | NHP | AA | 22 | 136 | 139 | 11.1 | .283 | -1.9 | C(34): 5.0 | 1.6 |
| 2018 | BUF | AAA | 23 | 369 | 94 | 8.6 | .281 | 1.6 | C(73): 15.0 | 2.9 |
| 2018 | TOR | MLB | 23 | 33 | 95 | 3.3 | .350 | 0.3 | C(11): 0.7 | 0.2 |
| 2019 | BUF | AAA | 24 | 277 | 77 | 3.4 | .276 | -3.8 | C(71): 4.2 | 0.7 |
| 2019 | TOR | MLB | 24 | 105 | 107 | 6.4 | .324 | 0.6 | C(30): 5.0 | 1.2 |
| 2020 | TOR | MLB | 25 | 385 | 83 | 9.2 | .268 | -0.4 | C 13 | 2.3 |

**Reese McGuire, continued**

**Batted Ball Distribution**

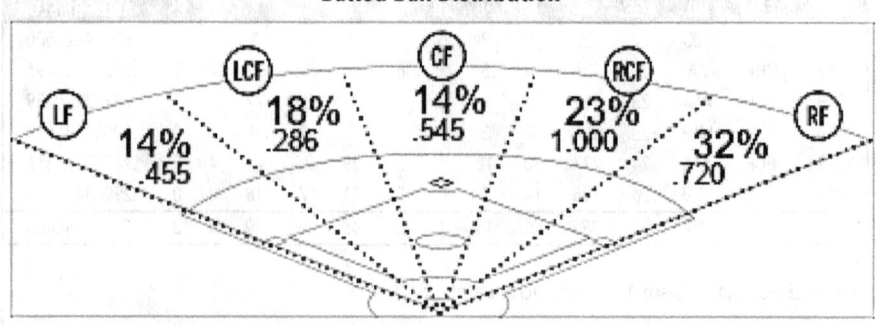

**Strike Zone vs LHP**  **Strike Zone vs RHP**

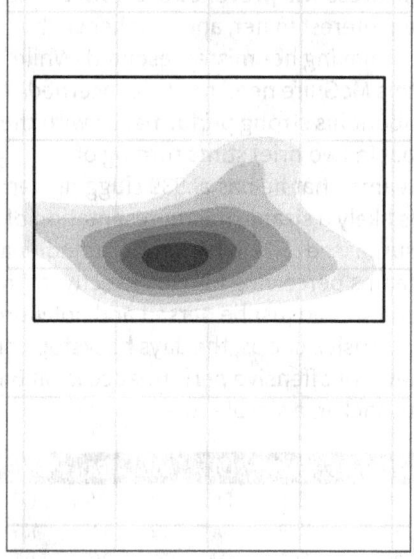

## Billy McKinney  OF

Born: 08/23/94   Age: 25   Bats: L   Throws: L
Height: 6'1"   Weight: 205   Origin: Round 1, 2013 Draft (#24 overall)

| YEAR | TEAM | LVL | AGE | PA | R | 2B | 3B | HR | RBI | BB | K | SB | CS | AVG/OBP/SLG |
|---|---|---|---|---|---|---|---|---|---|---|---|---|---|---|
| 2017 | TRN | AA | 22 | 276 | 34 | 16 | 4 | 6 | 29 | 30 | 45 | 2 | 1 | .250/.339/.431 |
| 2017 | SWB | AAA | 22 | 224 | 32 | 13 | 3 | 10 | 35 | 9 | 49 | 0 | 0 | .306/.336/.541 |
| 2018 | SWB | AAA | 23 | 234 | 27 | 8 | 5 | 13 | 32 | 21 | 56 | 0 | 0 | .226/.299/.495 |
| 2018 | BUF | AAA | 23 | 72 | 10 | 3 | 2 | 3 | 8 | 8 | 16 | 0 | 0 | .203/.292/.453 |
| 2018 | NYA | MLB | 23 | 4 | 0 | 0 | 0 | 0 | 0 | 0 | 1 | 0 | 0 | .250/.250/.250 |
| 2018 | TOR | MLB | 23 | 128 | 14 | 7 | 0 | 6 | 13 | 11 | 32 | 1 | 0 | .252/.320/.470 |
| 2019 | BUF | AAA | 24 | 154 | 17 | 8 | 4 | 4 | 20 | 22 | 25 | 1 | 1 | .271/.383/.488 |
| 2019 | TOR | MLB | 24 | 276 | 37 | 14 | 1 | 12 | 28 | 19 | 73 | 0 | 2 | .215/.274/.422 |
| 2020 | TOR | MLB | 25 | 175 | 21 | 9 | 1 | 8 | 25 | 15 | 44 | 0 | 0 | .242/.314/.473 |

Comparables: Jorge Bonifacio, Clint Frazier, Wil Myers

William McKinley was the 25th U.S. President, assassinated in 1901 by anarchist Leon Czolgosz. As he succumbed to gangrene, his wife Ida is said to have cried, "I want to go too," to which McKinley replied, "we are all going" (and then went). Another William, McKinney's MLB career is still in its incipient stages, much as McKinley's presidency was when he was twice shot. It was the second bullet, which doctors could not locate in 25's abdomen, which sprung his mortal coil. After sputtering in his most extended opportunity yet, half the Jays' return for J.A. Happ is at risk of his career falling into sepsis—the two bullets acting on him are his lack of positional versatility and his below-average batting at the MLB level. In cases of sepsis, there is only so much time before the damage becomes irreversible, and the lefty's chances of healing his career are running sparse.

| YEAR | TEAM | LVL | AGE | PA | DRC+ | VORP | BABIP | BRR | FRAA | WARP |
|---|---|---|---|---|---|---|---|---|---|---|
| 2017 | TRN | AA | 22 | 276 | 103 | 13.2 | .277 | 0.3 | RF(50): 12.3, LF(10): -1.1 | 2.2 |
| 2017 | SWB | AAA | 22 | 224 | 128 | 12.6 | .353 | -0.7 | LF(26): 0.1, RF(26): 1.6 | 1.2 |
| 2018 | SWB | AAA | 23 | 234 | 99 | 7.5 | .245 | 0.5 | RF(32): -1.8, CF(12): 1.6 | 0.4 |
| 2018 | BUF | AAA | 23 | 72 | 102 | 0.9 | .222 | 0.4 | RF(14): 3.3, 1B(4): 0.0 | 0.6 |
| 2018 | NYA | MLB | 23 | 4 | 98 | -0.1 | .333 | 0.0 | LF(2): -0.2 | 0.0 |
| 2018 | TOR | MLB | 23 | 128 | 99 | 2.8 | .295 | -1.9 | LF(26): -0.3, RF(13): -0.3 | 0.0 |
| 2019 | BUF | AAA | 24 | 154 | 119 | 7.9 | .307 | -1.5 | LF(16): 1.1, RF(8): 2.2 | 0.7 |
| 2019 | TOR | MLB | 24 | 276 | 80 | -0.4 | .250 | -0.3 | RF(43): 0.0, LF(29): -2.2 | -0.3 |
| 2020 | TOR | MLB | 25 | 175 | 100 | 2.8 | .282 | -0.4 | RF 1, LF -1 | 0.3 |

*Billy McKinney, continued*

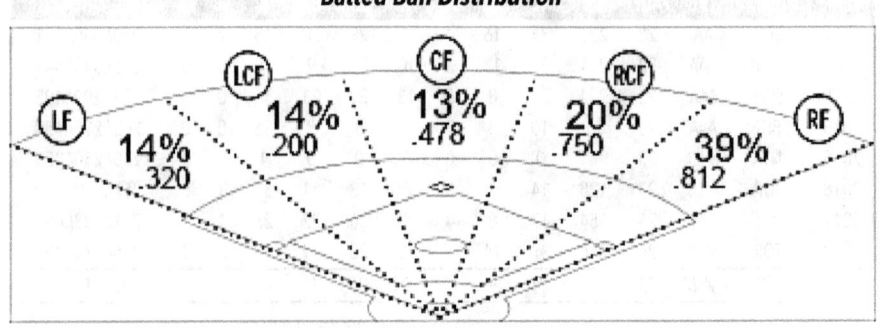

**Batted Ball Distribution**

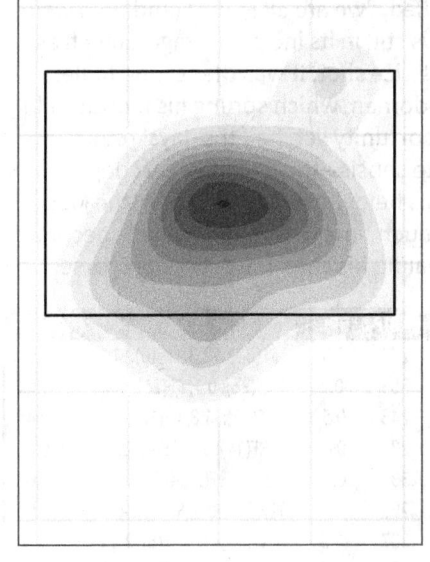

**Strike Zone vs LHP**

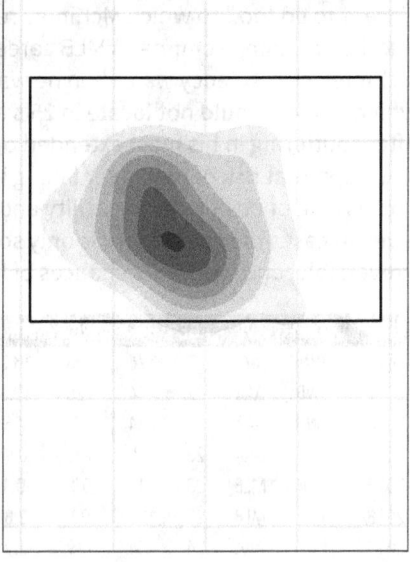

**Strike Zone vs RHP**

### Joe Panik  2B

Born: 10/30/90   Age: 29   Bats: L   Throws: R
Height: 6'1"   Weight: 200   Origin: Round 1, 2011 Draft (#29 overall)

| YEAR | TEAM | LVL | AGE | PA | R | 2B | 3B | HR | RBI | BB | K | SB | CS | AVG/OBP/SLG |
|---|---|---|---|---|---|---|---|---|---|---|---|---|---|---|
| 2017 | SFN | MLB | 26 | 573 | 60 | 28 | 5 | 10 | 53 | 46 | 54 | 4 | 1 | .288/.347/.421 |
| 2018 | SFN | MLB | 27 | 392 | 38 | 14 | 1 | 4 | 24 | 26 | 30 | 4 | 2 | .254/.307/.332 |
| 2019 | SFN | MLB | 28 | 388 | 33 | 17 | 1 | 3 | 27 | 36 | 38 | 4 | 2 | .235/.310/.317 |
| 2019 | NYN | MLB | 28 | 103 | 17 | 4 | 1 | 2 | 12 | 7 | 9 | 0 | 0 | .277/.333/.404 |
| 2020 | NYN | MLB | 29 | 251 | 24 | 11 | 1 | 5 | 25 | 21 | 28 | 2 | 1 | .248/.317/.367 |

Comparables: Rich Rollins, Johnny Giavotella, Justin Turner

The former Giant second baseman finally fulfilled Sandy Alderson's "Panic City" proclamation from 2015 when he came over to the Mets in August and turned New York into Panik Citi by hitting .342 and scoring 10 runs over his first 12 games with the team. It was a really fun homecoming at first as Panik had been drafted out of St. John's University—just a few miles or 45 minutes of traffic up the Grand Central—but the party was short-lived, as he returned to the bench once Robinson Canó returned to the lineup in early September. All in all, he was and is a perfectly cromulent bench piece who should not be stretched into everyday work again.

| YEAR | TEAM | LVL | AGE | PA | DRC+ | VORP | BABIP | BRR | FRAA | WARP |
|---|---|---|---|---|---|---|---|---|---|---|
| 2017 | SFN | MLB | 26 | 573 | 100 | 26.3 | .301 | 0.9 | 2B(137): -7.5 | 1.1 |
| 2018 | SFN | MLB | 27 | 392 | 86 | 1.6 | .265 | 1.0 | 2B(94): 4.3, 1B(1): 0.1 | 1.1 |
| 2019 | SFN | MLB | 28 | 388 | 86 | 5.9 | .254 | -0.5 | 2B(90): 5.0 | 1.0 |
| 2019 | NYN | MLB | 28 | 103 | 91 | 2.3 | .289 | -0.1 | 2B(28): -1.4 | 0.1 |
| 2020 | NYN | MLB | 29 | 251 | 83 | 2.6 | .266 | 0.2 | 2B -1, 1B 0 | 0.2 |

*Joe Panik, continued*

**Batted Ball Distribution**

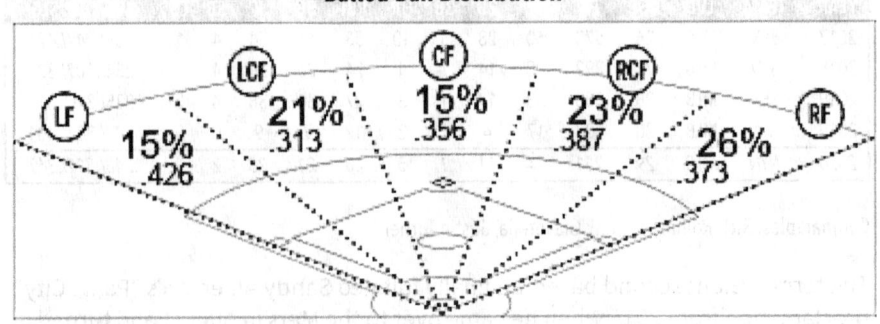

**Strike Zone vs LHP**          **Strike Zone vs RHP**

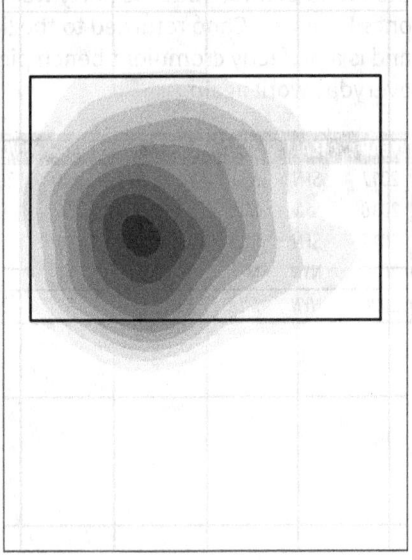

## Travis Shaw  3B

Born: 04/16/90  Age: 30  Bats: L  Throws: R
Height: 6'4"  Weight: 230  Origin: Round 9, 2011 Draft (#292 overall)

| YEAR | TEAM | LVL | AGE | PA | R | 2B | 3B | HR | RBI | BB | K | SB | CS | AVG/OBP/SLG |
|---|---|---|---|---|---|---|---|---|---|---|---|---|---|---|
| 2017 | MIL | MLB | 27 | 606 | 84 | 34 | 1 | 31 | 101 | 60 | 138 | 10 | 0 | .273/.349/.513 |
| 2018 | MIL | MLB | 28 | 587 | 73 | 23 | 0 | 32 | 86 | 78 | 108 | 5 | 2 | .241/.345/.480 |
| 2019 | SAN | AAA | 29 | 174 | 27 | 4 | 0 | 12 | 33 | 36 | 37 | 3 | 1 | .286/.437/.586 |
| 2019 | MIL | MLB | 29 | 270 | 22 | 5 | 0 | 7 | 16 | 36 | 89 | 0 | 0 | .157/.281/.270 |
| 2020 | TOR | MLB | 30 | 455 | 62 | 19 | 1 | 26 | 71 | 54 | 132 | 4 | 1 | .241/.337/.488 |

Comparables: Erubiel Durazo, Norm Zauchin, Freddie Freeman

The 10th percentile PECOTA projections on our website are as close as the system gets to providing a "worst-case scenario" for any given player. For Shaw, coming off a couple borderline All-Star seasons, his 10th percentile OPS was .678. You could talk yourself into it by envision his strikeout issues flaring up, or his power numbers dipping as his bat speed eroded, or some combination thereof. Both of those things (and more) happened, leaving him more than 100 points below that supposed floor. Shaw's approach also fell apart, and even a 42-game stint in the Pacific Coast League couldn't revive it. Power can be fickle, but a smart approach is supposed to transcend slumps. Shaw's didn't, and while he's been too good to give up on, it's possible that his collapse is indicative of a legitimate decline in skill.

| YEAR | TEAM | LVL | AGE | PA | DRC+ | VORP | BABIP | BRR | FRAA | WARP |
|---|---|---|---|---|---|---|---|---|---|---|
| 2017 | MIL | MLB | 27 | 606 | 114 | 40.9 | .312 | 3.2 | 3B(143): 0.9, 1B(1): 0.0 | 3.7 |
| 2018 | MIL | MLB | 28 | 587 | 120 | 43.5 | .242 | -0.7 | 3B(107): 1.8, 2B(39): -0.5 | 3.5 |
| 2019 | SAN | AAA | 29 | 174 | 161 | 21.6 | .299 | -2.1 | 3B(23): 1.0, 1B(10): 0.4 | 1.6 |
| 2019 | MIL | MLB | 29 | 270 | 71 | -0.2 | .216 | 0.1 | 3B(71): 2.3, 1B(6): 0.2 | 0.2 |
| 2020 | TOR | MLB | 30 | 455 | 109 | 14.9 | .291 | 0.3 | 1B 2, 3B 1 | 1.8 |

*Travis Shaw, continued*

**Batted Ball Distribution**

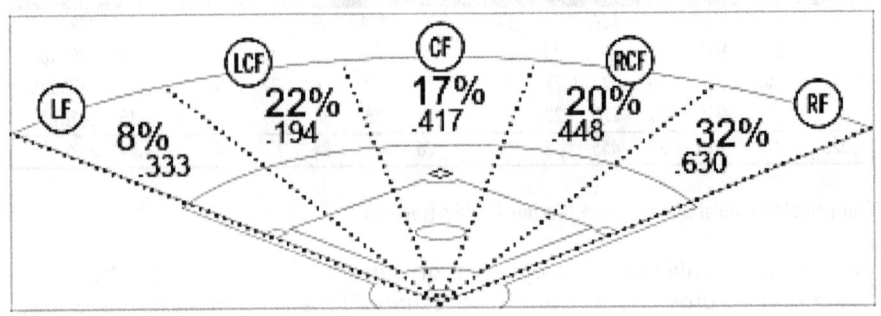

**Strike Zone vs LHP**       **Strike Zone vs RHP**

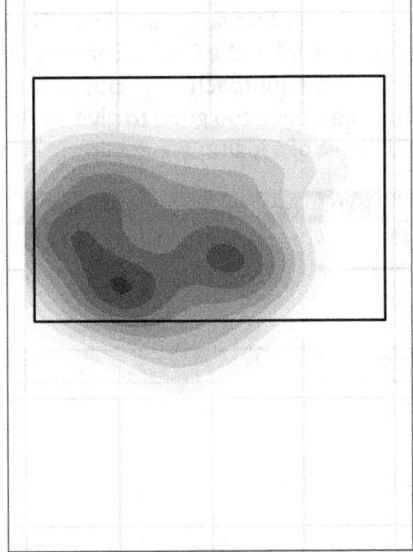

## Rowdy Tellez 1B

Born: 03/16/95  Age: 25  Bats: L  Throws: L
Height: 6'4"  Weight: 255  Origin: Round 30, 2013 Draft (#895 overall)

| YEAR | TEAM | LVL | AGE | PA | R | 2B | 3B | HR | RBI | BB | K | SB | CS | AVG/OBP/SLG |
|---|---|---|---|---|---|---|---|---|---|---|---|---|---|---|
| 2017 | BUF | AAA | 22 | 501 | 45 | 29 | 1 | 6 | 56 | 47 | 94 | 6 | 1 | .222/.295/.333 |
| 2018 | BUF | AAA | 23 | 444 | 43 | 22 | 0 | 13 | 50 | 40 | 74 | 7 | 4 | .270/.340/.425 |
| 2018 | TOR | MLB | 23 | 73 | 10 | 9 | 0 | 4 | 14 | 2 | 21 | 0 | 0 | .314/.329/.614 |
| 2019 | BUF | AAA | 24 | 109 | 20 | 9 | 0 | 7 | 21 | 14 | 25 | 0 | 0 | .366/.450/.688 |
| 2019 | TOR | MLB | 24 | 409 | 49 | 19 | 0 | 21 | 54 | 29 | 116 | 1 | 1 | .227/.293/.449 |
| 2020 | TOR | MLB | 25 | 385 | 51 | 17 | 0 | 23 | 61 | 32 | 104 | 2 | 1 | .246/.316/.496 |

Comparables: Ronald Guzmán, Steve Bilko, Dominic Smith

On September 25th, Tellez' biggest young fan, family friend Emmet Cooper, told him he had to hit a home run. Tellez hit two. Maybe this year, Cooper will tell the 25-year-old to take a walk. Tellez racked up one base on balls for every four strikeouts he tallied in 2019, putting him squarely below-average as a hitter despite his 21 long flies. To be more than a simple holdover until the next good edition of the Blue Jays, Tellez will need to bring more of the disciplined approach he's shown in the upper minors—or just keep hitting dingers on command.

| YEAR | TEAM | LVL | AGE | PA | DRC+ | VORP | BABIP | BRR | FRAA | WARP |
|---|---|---|---|---|---|---|---|---|---|---|
| 2017 | BUF | AAA | 22 | 501 | 79 | -11.6 | .264 | -0.6 | 1B(115): 1.8 | -0.4 |
| 2018 | BUF | AAA | 23 | 444 | 126 | 9.5 | .298 | -0.8 | 1B(107): -3.0 | 1.2 |
| 2018 | TOR | MLB | 23 | 73 | 101 | 5.3 | .391 | -0.1 | 1B(17): -0.4 | 0.1 |
| 2019 | BUF | AAA | 24 | 109 | 176 | 12.2 | .435 | -1.6 | 1B(25): 1.9 | 1.1 |
| 2019 | TOR | MLB | 24 | 409 | 91 | 1.7 | .267 | -1.1 | 1B(57): 4.3 | 0.5 |
| 2020 | TOR | MLB | 25 | 385 | 103 | 7.4 | .284 | -0.5 | 1B 1 | 0.8 |

*Rowdy Tellez, continued*

**Batted Ball Distribution**

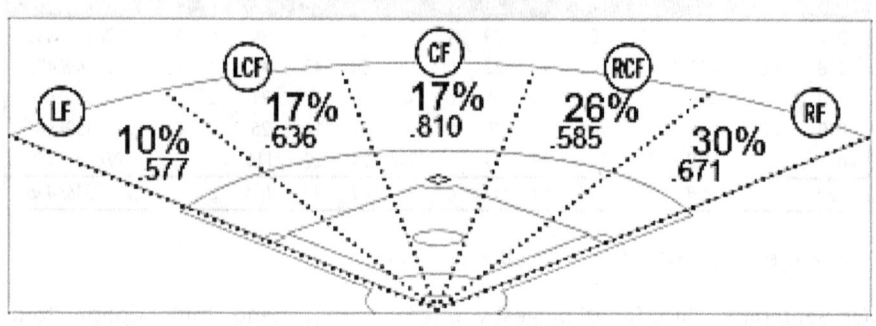

**Strike Zone vs LHP**            **Strike Zone vs RHP**

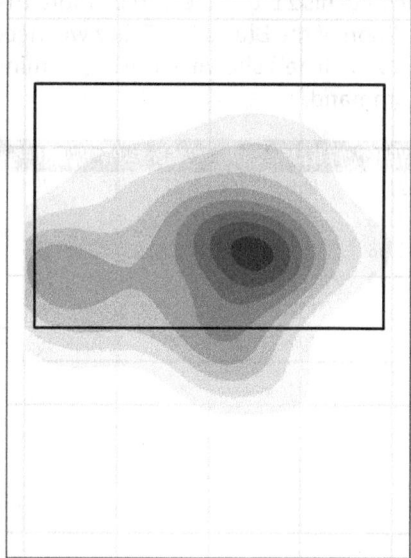

## Chase Anderson  RHP

Born: 11/30/87   Age: 32   Bats: R   Throws: R
Height: 6'1"   Weight: 200   Origin: Round 9, 2009 Draft (#276 overall)

| YEAR | TEAM | LVL | AGE | W | L | SV | G | GS | IP | H | HR | BB/9 | K/9 | K | GB% | BABIP |
|---|---|---|---|---|---|---|---|---|---|---|---|---|---|---|---|---|
| 2017 | MIL | MLB | 29 | 12 | 4 | 0 | 25 | 25 | 141$^1$ | 113 | 14 | 2.6 | 8.5 | 133 | 41% | .265 |
| 2018 | MIL | MLB | 30 | 9 | 8 | 0 | 30 | 30 | 158 | 131 | 30 | 3.2 | 7.3 | 128 | 36% | .239 |
| 2019 | MIL | MLB | 31 | 8 | 4 | 0 | 32 | 27 | 139 | 126 | 23 | 3.2 | 8.0 | 124 | 36% | .266 |
| 2020 | TOR | MLB | 32 | 8 | 7 | 0 | 23 | 23 | 120 | 117 | 25 | 3.4 | 8.0 | 107 | 36% | .275 |

Comparables: Chad Bettis, Joe Kelly, Kyle Gibson

Anderson has now surrendered 113 homers over the past five seasons, ranking him 23rd among big-league pitchers. (For reference, he's 43rd in innings during that span.) He has a tantalizing skillset, including a mid-90s fastball and four secondary pitches. The best one, the changeup, is a true swing-and-miss offering (16 percent whiff rate) and protects him from platoon-heavy lineups. But that home-run problem lingers, and has been the difference between a potential mid-rotation starter and somebody who has to scrap to hang onto a rotation spot. The Blue Jays hope a change of scenery can reverse his fortunes—at least long enough to drum up trade interest.

| YEAR | TEAM | LVL | AGE | WHIP | ERA | DRA | WARP | MPH | FB% | WHF | CSP |
|---|---|---|---|---|---|---|---|---|---|---|---|
| 2017 | MIL | MLB | 29 | 1.09 | 2.74 | 4.13 | 2.3 | 95.4 | 52.5 | 11.5 | 47.6 |
| 2018 | MIL | MLB | 30 | 1.19 | 3.93 | 5.52 | -0.4 | 94.5 | 53.5 | 10.3 | 46.9 |
| 2019 | MIL | MLB | 31 | 1.27 | 4.21 | 4.84 | 1.4 | 95.4 | 50.8 | 11.9 | 47.6 |
| 2020 | TOR | MLB | 32 | 1.35 | 4.96 | 4.89 | 0.9 | 94.1 | 51.7 | 11.1 | 47 |

# Toronto Blue Jays 2020

**Chase Anderson, continued**

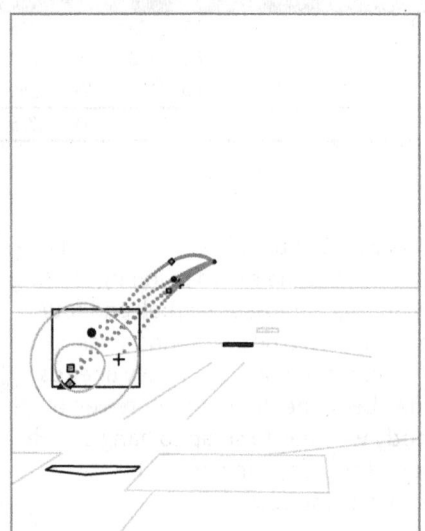
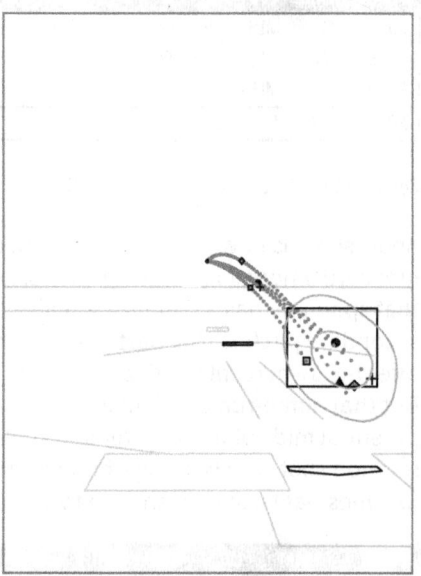

| Type | Frequency | Velocity | H Movement | V Movement |
|---|---|---|---|---|
| ● Fastball | 43.2% | 93.6 [103] | -7.2 [99] | -13 [108] |
| ☐ Sinker | 7.5% | 93.4 [104] | -11.7 [106] | -15.6 [117] |
| + Cutter | 14.8% | 90.9 [114] | 1.5 [98] | -18.1 [122] |
| ▲ Changeup | 24.2% | 82.9 [91] | -14.8 [83] | -25.4 [106] |
| ✕ Splitter | | | | |
| ▽ Slider | | | | |
| ◇ Curveball | 10.3% | 78 [98] | 7 [98] | -52.2 [90] |
| ✦ Slow Curveball | | | | |
| ✱ Knuckleball | | | | |
| ▼ Screwball | | | | |

## Anthony Bass  RHP

Born: 11/01/87  Age: 32  Bats: R  Throws: R
Height: 6'2"  Weight: 200  Origin: Round 5, 2008 Draft (#165 overall)

| YEAR | TEAM | LVL | AGE | W | L | SV | G | GS | IP | H | HR | BB/9 | K/9 | K | GB% | BABIP |
|---|---|---|---|---|---|---|---|---|---|---|---|---|---|---|---|---|
| 2017 | RNG | RK | 29 | 0 | 1 | 0 | 3 | 2 | 9 | 11 | 1 | 2.0 | 9.0 | 9 | 52% | .385 |
| 2017 | ROU | AAA | 29 | 3 | 4 | 0 | 18 | 12 | 75$^1$ | 79 | 7 | 3.3 | 10.4 | 87 | 43% | .358 |
| 2017 | TEX | MLB | 29 | 0 | 0 | 0 | 2 | 0 | 5$^2$ | 14 | 1 | 0.0 | 1.6 | 1 | 47% | .448 |
| 2018 | IOW | AAA | 30 | 0 | 3 | 3 | 27 | 0 | 32 | 34 | 3 | 1.7 | 7.0 | 25 | 53% | .307 |
| 2018 | CHN | MLB | 30 | 0 | 0 | 0 | 16 | 0 | 15$^1$ | 18 | 1 | 1.8 | 8.2 | 14 | 53% | .386 |
| 2019 | LOU | AAA | 31 | 1 | 1 | 9 | 19 | 0 | 20$^1$ | 13 | 1 | 2.7 | 8.4 | 19 | 55% | .222 |
| 2019 | SEA | MLB | 31 | 2 | 4 | 5 | 44 | 0 | 48 | 30 | 5 | 3.2 | 8.1 | 43 | 55% | .203 |
| 2020 | TOR | MLB | 32 | 3 | 3 | 7 | 58 | 0 | 62 | 63 | 9 | 3.3 | 8.3 | 57 | 55% | .304 |

Comparables: Brandon League, Al McBean, Neil Allen

In the sea of Anthony Bass-types that floated through the Mariners bullpen in 2019 was Bass himself, who quietly turned in a sufficient season for a team that surely appreciated even the slightest semblance of consistency. Bass' average fastball velocity sat north of 95 mph for the first time as a big leaguer, and he posted career-best marks in both WHIP and DRA. His multi-year journey to find a stable role in a big-league 'pen may actually have a happy ending after all, as he was scooped up by the Blue Jays in November. He'll compete for the role of setup man to Ken Giles.

| YEAR | TEAM | LVL | AGE | WHIP | ERA | DRA | WARP | MPH | FB% | WHF | CSP |
|---|---|---|---|---|---|---|---|---|---|---|---|
| 2017 | RNG | RK | 29 | 1.44 | 4.00 | 3.74 | 0.2 | | | | |
| 2017 | ROU | AAA | 29 | 1.42 | 4.18 | 5.01 | 0.5 | | | | |
| 2017 | TEX | MLB | 29 | 2.47 | 14.29 | 7.65 | -0.2 | 94.6 | 63.1 | 8.1 | 46.9 |
| 2018 | IOW | AAA | 30 | 1.25 | 3.38 | 4.36 | 0.3 | | | | |
| 2018 | CHN | MLB | 30 | 1.37 | 2.93 | 4.77 | 0.0 | 96.1 | 68.4 | 8.6 | 48.4 |
| 2019 | LOU | AAA | 31 | 0.93 | 2.21 | 2.71 | 0.7 | | | | |
| 2019 | SEA | MLB | 31 | 0.98 | 3.56 | 3.43 | 1.0 | 97.2 | 52.7 | 12.3 | 43 |
| 2020 | TOR | MLB | 32 | 1.38 | 4.50 | 4.52 | 0.5 | 95.9 | 56 | 11.2 | 45.4 |

## Anthony Bass, continued

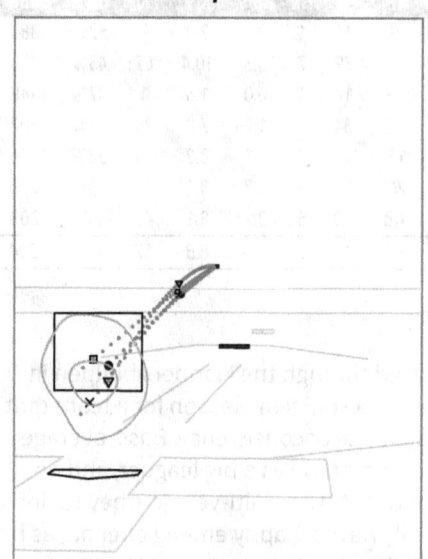
**Pitch Shape vs LHH**

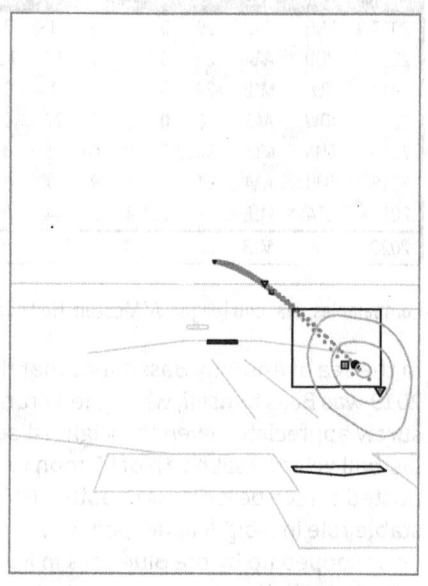
**Pitch Shape vs RHH**

| Type | Frequency | Velocity | H Movement | V Movement |
|---|---|---|---|---|
| ● Fastball | 11.8% | 95.8 [110] | -8.6 [92] | -13.7 [106] |
| □ Sinker | 40.9% | 95.6 [115] | -12 [104] | -15.3 [118] |
| + Cutter | | | | |
| ▲ Changeup | | | | |
| ✕ Splitter | 14.3% | 86.9 [108] | -5 [111] | -25 [114] |
| ▽ Slider | 33.1% | 87.6 [113] | 5.1 [100] | -30.8 [106] |
| ◇ Curveball | | | | |
| ✦ Slow Curveball | | | | |
| ✱ Knuckleball | | | | |
| ▼ Screwball | | | | |

## Buddy Boshers  LHP

Born: 05/09/88  Age: 32  Bats: L  Throws: L
Height: 6'3"  Weight: 222  Origin: Round 4, 2008 Draft (#139 overall)

| YEAR | TEAM | LVL | AGE | W | L | SV | G | GS | IP | H | HR | BB/9 | K/9 | K | GB% | BABIP |
|---|---|---|---|---|---|---|---|---|---|---|---|---|---|---|---|---|
| 2017 | ROC | AAA | 29 | 0 | 0 | 0 | 18 | 0 | 14$^2$ | 16 | 1 | 4.9 | 9.2 | 15 | 52% | .366 |
| 2017 | MIN | MLB | 29 | 1 | 0 | 0 | 38 | 0 | 35 | 37 | 7 | 2.6 | 7.2 | 28 | 47% | .283 |
| 2018 | FRE | AAA | 30 | 2 | 1 | 4 | 41 | 0 | 51 | 48 | 5 | 2.6 | 9.7 | 55 | 49% | .319 |
| 2018 | IND | AAA | 30 | 0 | 1 | 1 | 7 | 0 | 6 | 6 | 0 | 4.5 | 10.5 | 7 | 47% | .353 |
| 2019 | BUF | AAA | 31 | 0 | 2 | 5 | 25 | 0 | 32$^1$ | 27 | 3 | 3.9 | 9.7 | 35 | 41% | .289 |
| 2019 | TOR | MLB | 31 | 0 | 3 | 0 | 28 | 1 | 20 | 20 | 3 | 4.5 | 11.7 | 26 | 46% | .333 |
| 2020 | TOR | MLB | 32 | 2 | 2 | 0 | 33 | 0 | 35 | 35 | 6 | 3.7 | 9.5 | 37 | 45% | .308 |

Comparables: Lucas Luetge, Kevin Chapman, Sam Freeman

With a name that sounds less like an MLB reliever and more like a new character on the coming *Blue's Clues* reboot, Boshers has now pitched in four of the last seven seasons as a lefty specialist—he has faced 200 left-handed batters in his career compared to just 259 righties. Boshers actually posted a reverse split in his two months in Toronto, which would be more reason for concern had he not been league-average against right-handed batters (compared to his last MLB stint, when they posted a collective OPS of .904 against him). More pressing for his hopes of appearing in the bigs in back-to-back seasons, in 13 of Boshers' 28 appearances for Toronto he faced two batters or less. Still, the 32-year-old posted the best strikeout rate of his career and that will give him at least a fighting chance to avoid extinction.

| YEAR | TEAM | LVL | AGE | WHIP | ERA | DRA | WARP | MPH | FB% | WHF | CSP |
|---|---|---|---|---|---|---|---|---|---|---|---|
| 2017 | ROC | AAA | 29 | 1.64 | 3.68 | 5.75 | -0.1 | | | | |
| 2017 | MIN | MLB | 29 | 1.34 | 4.89 | 3.85 | 0.5 | 91.8 | 48.9 | 11.4 | 46.6 |
| 2018 | FRE | AAA | 30 | 1.24 | 3.18 | 3.78 | 0.8 | | | | |
| 2018 | IND | AAA | 30 | 1.50 | 4.50 | 4.43 | 0.0 | | | | |
| 2019 | BUF | AAA | 31 | 1.27 | 2.78 | 3.88 | 0.7 | | | | |
| 2019 | TOR | MLB | 31 | 1.50 | 4.05 | 4.59 | 0.2 | 94.4 | 39.6 | 9.1 | 46.8 |
| 2020 | TOR | MLB | 32 | 1.40 | 4.68 | 4.66 | 0.2 | 92.1 | 43.5 | 10.1 | 46.3 |

# Toronto Blue Jays 2020

**Buddy Boshers, continued**

### Pitch Shape vs LHH

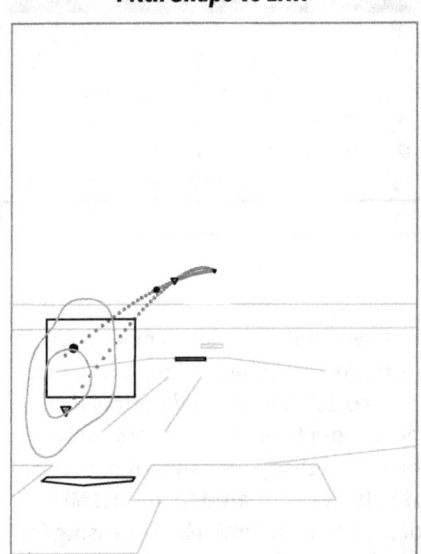

### Pitch Shape vs RHH

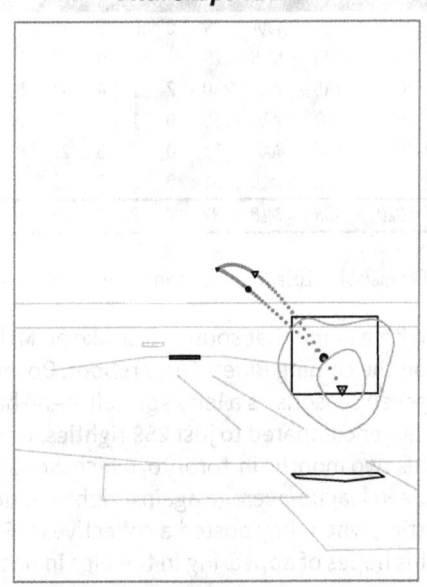

| Type | Frequency | Velocity | H Movement | V Movement |
|---|---|---|---|---|
| ● Fastball | 39.6% | 92.8 [101] | 9.4 [88] | -15.7 [101] |
| ☐ Sinker | | | | |
| + Cutter | | | | |
| ▲ Changeup | 6.8% | 84.5 [97] | 11.3 [99] | -28.1 [98] |
| ✕ Splitter | | | | |
| ▽ Slider | 53.6% | 80.5 [84] | -3.3 [93] | -46.9 [60] |
| ◇ Curveball | | | | |
| ✦ Slow Curveball | | | | |
| ✱ Knuckleball | | | | |
| ▼ Screwball | | | | |

## Clay Buchholz  RHP

Born: 08/14/84  Age: 35  Bats: L  Throws: R
Height: 6'3"  Weight: 190  Origin: Round 1, 2005 Draft (#42 overall)

| YEAR | TEAM | LVL | AGE | W | L | SV | G | GS | IP | H | HR | BB/9 | K/9 | K | GB% | BABIP |
|---|---|---|---|---|---|---|---|---|---|---|---|---|---|---|---|---|
| 2017 | PHI | MLB | 32 | 0 | 1 | 0 | 2 | 2 | 7$^1$ | 16 | 1 | 3.7 | 6.1 | 5 | 31% | .484 |
| 2018 | VIS | A+ | 33 | 1 | 0 | 0 | 1 | 1 | 6 | 4 | 1 | 1.5 | 9.0 | 6 | 47% | .214 |
| 2018 | OMA | AAA | 33 | 1 | 0 | 0 | 2 | 2 | 11$^1$ | 9 | 2 | 4.0 | 3.2 | 4 | 55% | .194 |
| 2018 | RNO | AAA | 33 | 0 | 1 | 0 | 2 | 2 | 11$^2$ | 12 | 0 | 3.9 | 7.7 | 10 | 40% | .324 |
| 2018 | ARI | MLB | 33 | 7 | 2 | 0 | 16 | 16 | 98$^1$ | 80 | 9 | 2.0 | 7.4 | 81 | 43% | .256 |
| 2019 | TOR | MLB | 34 | 2 | 5 | 0 | 12 | 12 | 59 | 72 | 13 | 2.4 | 5.9 | 39 | 46% | .321 |
| *2020* | *TOR* | *MLB* | *35* | *2* | *2* | *0* | *33* | *0* | *35* | *37* | *7* | *2.9* | *6.7* | *26* | *44%* | *.287* |

Comparables: Ervin Santana, Matt Garza, Jhoulys Chacín

"Man crafted from clay" is one of the most common creation myths, and humanity's fragility in relation to the gods an expected consequence. Buchholz has exemplified that fragility over the last three seasons, totaling just thirty starts and never crossing 100 innings after five consecutive seasons breaking that threshold. Still, even in a season again limited by injury, Buchholz played the Prometheus role, providing leadership and shelter to young charges—after a ball popped out of Billy McKinley's glove in a September game and led to several runs, Buchholz refused the outfielder's apology. Even as he struggled through season that must have felt like being chained to a rock and having his liver pecked out, the 34-year-old was an important presence to the developing squad.

| YEAR | TEAM | LVL | AGE | WHIP | ERA | DRA | WARP | MPH | FB% | WHF | CSP |
|---|---|---|---|---|---|---|---|---|---|---|---|
| 2017 | PHI | MLB | 32 | 2.59 | 12.27 | 6.77 | -0.1 | 92.7 | 65.2 | 6.5 | 49.7 |
| 2018 | VIS | A+ | 33 | 0.83 | 3.00 | 3.35 | 0.1 | | | | |
| 2018 | OMA | AAA | 33 | 1.24 | 1.59 | 5.07 | 0.1 | | | | |
| 2018 | RNO | AAA | 33 | 1.46 | 5.40 | 4.73 | 0.1 | | | | |
| 2018 | ARI | MLB | 33 | 1.04 | 2.01 | 3.74 | 1.8 | 92.0 | 65.9 | 10.5 | 50.4 |
| 2019 | TOR | MLB | 34 | 1.49 | 6.56 | 8.00 | -1.4 | 91.8 | 62.8 | 9.7 | 47.5 |
| *2020* | *TOR* | *MLB* | *35* | *1.39* | *5.09* | *5.09* | *0.0* | *90.7* | *63.3* | *9.8* | *48.1* |

# Toronto Blue Jays 2020

**Clay Buchholz, continued**

**Pitch Shape vs LHH**          **Pitch Shape vs RHH**

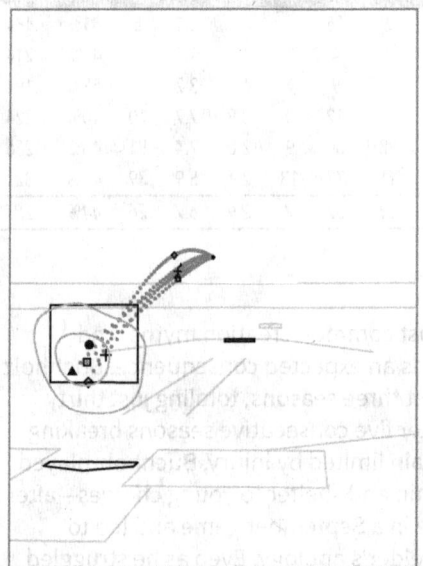 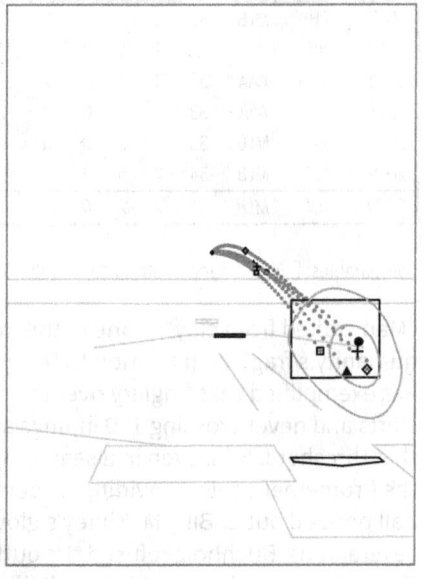

| Type | Frequency | Velocity | H Movement | V Movement |
|---|---|---|---|---|
| ● Fastball | 14.3% | 90.1 [93] | -7.7 [96] | -15.9 [100] |
| □ Sinker | 20.2% | 89.5 [84] | -12.2 [103] | -20.1 [101] |
| + Cutter | 28.2% | 84.8 [76] | 2.5 [104] | -26.9 [89] |
| ▲ Changeup | 19.7% | 77 [70] | -8.8 [111] | -34.5 [79] |
| ✕ Splitter | | | | |
| ▽ Slider | | | | |
| ◇ Curveball | 17.4% | 75.5 [90] | 12.3 [119] | -53.3 [88] |
| ✜ Slow Curveball | | | | |
| ✱ Knuckleball | | | | |
| ▼ Screwball | | | | |

## Wilmer Font  RHP
Born: 05/24/90  Age: 30  Bats: R  Throws: R
Height: 6'4"  Weight: 250  Origin: International Free Agent, 2006

| YEAR | TEAM | LVL | AGE | W | L | SV | G | GS | IP | H | HR | BB/9 | K/9 | K | GB% | BABIP |
|---|---|---|---|---|---|---|---|---|---|---|---|---|---|---|---|---|
| 2017 | OKL | AAA | 27 | 10 | 8 | 0 | 25 | 25 | 134$^1$ | 114 | 11 | 2.3 | 11.9 | 178 | 39% | .315 |
| 2017 | LAN | MLB | 27 | 0 | 0 | 0 | 3 | 0 | 3$^2$ | 7 | 2 | 9.8 | 7.4 | 3 | 27% | .385 |
| 2018 | LAN | MLB | 28 | 0 | 2 | 0 | 6 | 0 | 10$^1$ | 18 | 5 | 0.9 | 6.1 | 7 | 42% | .371 |
| 2018 | OAK | MLB | 28 | 0 | 0 | 0 | 4 | 0 | 6$^2$ | 13 | 5 | 5.4 | 12.1 | 9 | 33% | .421 |
| 2018 | TBA | MLB | 28 | 2 | 1 | 0 | 9 | 5 | 27 | 15 | 2 | 3.7 | 6.7 | 20 | 45% | .178 |
| 2019 | TBA | MLB | 29 | 1 | 0 | 0 | 10 | 0 | 14 | 15 | 2 | 3.2 | 11.6 | 18 | 43% | .371 |
| 2019 | TOR | MLB | 29 | 2 | 3 | 0 | 23 | 14 | 39$^1$ | 34 | 7 | 2.5 | 12.1 | 53 | 35% | .300 |
| 2019 | NYN | MLB | 29 | 1 | 2 | 0 | 15 | 3 | 31 | 29 | 8 | 3.8 | 7.0 | 24 | 37% | .241 |
| 2020 | TOR | MLB | 30 | 3 | 3 | 0 | 52 | 0 | 56 | 50 | 11 | 3.1 | 9.2 | 57 | 38% | .274 |

Comparables: Matt Magill, Jhan Mariñez, Christian Garcia

Font's three-team 2019, by fonts. Fourteen innings through early May in Tampa Bay were Futura: widely used, though mainly for advertisement. After a trade to the Mets, three disastrous starts and twelve *fine* relief appearances over two months were Papyrus: brash, but maybe indicative of those who don't quite know what they're doing. A final 23 appearances in Toronto after a DFA, though, were Times New Roman: not the flashiest, but reliable and solidly above average. It remains to be seen if Font can remain as ubiquitous moving forward after a mixed bag of a season, but then we always tend to turn back to our recently-used fonts, and perhaps the same is true of GMs.

| YEAR | TEAM | LVL | AGE | WHIP | ERA | DRA | WARP | MPH | FB% | WHF | CSP |
|---|---|---|---|---|---|---|---|---|---|---|---|
| 2017 | OKL | AAA | 27 | 1.11 | 3.42 | 2.03 | 5.4 | | | | |
| 2017 | LAN | MLB | 27 | 3.00 | 17.18 | 7.49 | -0.1 | 97.0 | 68.1 | 11 | 44.3 |
| 2018 | LAN | MLB | 28 | 1.84 | 11.32 | 7.05 | -0.2 | 97.0 | 69.5 | 8.9 | 51.7 |
| 2018 | OAK | MLB | 28 | 2.55 | 14.85 | 3.80 | 0.1 | 97.7 | 68.5 | 13.6 | 41.8 |
| 2018 | TBA | MLB | 28 | 0.96 | 1.67 | 6.46 | -0.4 | 98.0 | 63.6 | 9.7 | 49 |
| 2019 | TBA | MLB | 29 | 1.43 | 5.79 | 4.85 | 0.1 | 97.1 | 50.9 | 15 | 47.1 |
| 2019 | TOR | MLB | 29 | 1.14 | 3.66 | 3.58 | 0.8 | 97.1 | 61.8 | 14.6 | 47.2 |
| 2019 | NYN | MLB | 29 | 1.35 | 4.94 | 6.66 | -0.4 | 97.0 | 58.5 | 11.2 | 47.9 |
| 2020 | TOR | MLB | 30 | 1.25 | 4.23 | 4.30 | 0.5 | 96.5 | 60.9 | 12.4 | 46.8 |

# Toronto Blue Jays 2020

**Wilmer Font, continued**

### Pitch Shape vs LHH

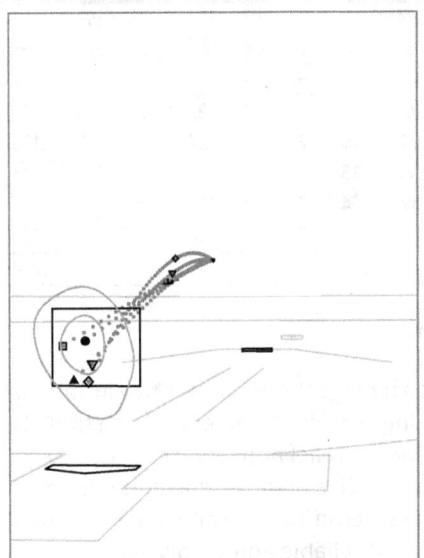

### Pitch Shape vs RHH

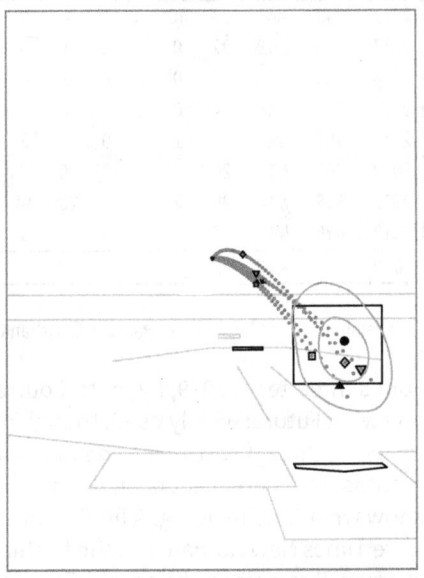

| Type | Frequency | Velocity | H Movement | V Movement |
|---|---|---|---|---|
| ● Fastball | 47.9% | 94.9 [107] | -4.6 [110] | -11.2 [112] |
| □ Sinker | 10.7% | 93.9 [107] | -11.3 [109] | -14.5 [121] |
| + Cutter | | | | |
| ▲ Changeup | 9.6% | 84.7 [98] | -6.2 [123] | -26.4 [103] |
| ✕ Splitter | | | | |
| ▽ Slider | 12.8% | 84.6 [101] | 5.8 [103] | -32.1 [103] |
| ◇ Curveball | 18.9% | 76.7 [94] | 9.2 [107] | -52.9 [89] |
| ⊕ Slow Curveball | | | | |
| ✱ Knuckleball | | | | |
| ▼ Screwball | | | | |

## Sam Gaviglio   RHP

Born: 05/22/90   Age: 30   Bats: R   Throws: R
Height: 6'2"   Weight: 205   Origin: Round 5, 2011 Draft (#170 overall)

| YEAR | TEAM | LVL | AGE | W | L | SV | G | GS | IP | H | HR | BB/9 | K/9 | K | GB% | BABIP |
|---|---|---|---|---|---|---|---|---|---|---|---|---|---|---|---|---|
| 2017 | TAC | AAA | 27 | 3 | 6 | 0 | 13 | 13 | 72 | 72 | 5 | 1.5 | 7.1 | 57 | 54% | .302 |
| 2017 | SEA | MLB | 27 | 3 | 5 | 0 | 12 | 11 | $62^1$ | 63 | 15 | 3.0 | 5.8 | 40 | 49% | .265 |
| 2017 | KCA | MLB | 27 | 1 | 0 | 0 | 4 | 2 | 12 | 13 | 1 | 3.8 | 6.8 | 9 | 56% | .316 |
| 2018 | BUF | AAA | 28 | 0 | 0 | 0 | 5 | 5 | 29 | 21 | 4 | 1.2 | 9.0 | 29 | 46% | .243 |
| 2018 | TOR | MLB | 28 | 3 | 10 | 0 | 26 | 24 | $123^2$ | 140 | 21 | 2.8 | 7.6 | 105 | 50% | .313 |
| 2019 | TOR | MLB | 29 | 4 | 2 | 0 | 52 | 0 | $95^2$ | 85 | 18 | 2.1 | 8.3 | 88 | 48% | .258 |
| 2020 | TOR | MLB | 30 | 3 | 3 | 0 | 64 | 0 | 68 | 71 | 13 | 2.6 | 8.2 | 62 | 48% | .297 |

Comparables: Chris Stratton, Brad Lincoln, Justin Haley

Having never been included in the massive pool of 21 starters Toronto used in 2019, you might assume his third big-league season was not a success. But actually, Gaviglio was worth five wins more than those 21 pitchers combined. The move to the bullpen agreed with the soft-tossing righty and the Blue Jays certainly got their money's worth out of him, as he was the only pitcher in baseball last year to throw 90 innings without making a start. For the first time using his slider more than his sinker, Gaviglio improved his strikeout rate without losing any of his low-walk, high-grounder profile. The rubber-armed righty who barely scratches 90 on the gun is not exactly a sought-after archetype in this era of a faceless and nameless legion of power arms, but as long as Gaviglio can work multiple innings at an above-average rate he'll have a home.

| YEAR | TEAM | LVL | AGE | WHIP | ERA | DRA | WARP | MPH | FB% | WHF | CSP |
|---|---|---|---|---|---|---|---|---|---|---|---|
| 2017 | TAC | AAA | 27 | 1.17 | 3.88 | 3.11 | 2.0 | | | | |
| 2017 | SEA | MLB | 27 | 1.35 | 4.62 | 5.69 | -0.1 | 90.6 | 56.6 | 7.3 | 50.3 |
| 2017 | KCA | MLB | 27 | 1.50 | 3.00 | 5.12 | 0.1 | 91.4 | 59.5 | 10 | 51.2 |
| 2018 | BUF | AAA | 28 | 0.86 | 1.86 | 3.12 | 0.8 | | | | |
| 2018 | TOR | MLB | 28 | 1.44 | 5.31 | 4.90 | 0.6 | 90.6 | 56 | 9.2 | 46.7 |
| 2019 | TOR | MLB | 29 | 1.12 | 4.61 | 4.12 | 1.3 | 91.4 | 42.6 | 12.5 | 47.8 |
| 2020 | TOR | MLB | 30 | 1.34 | 4.84 | 4.82 | 0.3 | 90.2 | 50.9 | 10.2 | 48 |

# Toronto Blue Jays 2020

**Sam Gaviglio, continued**

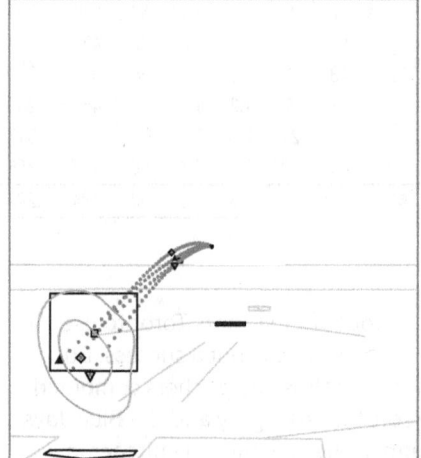
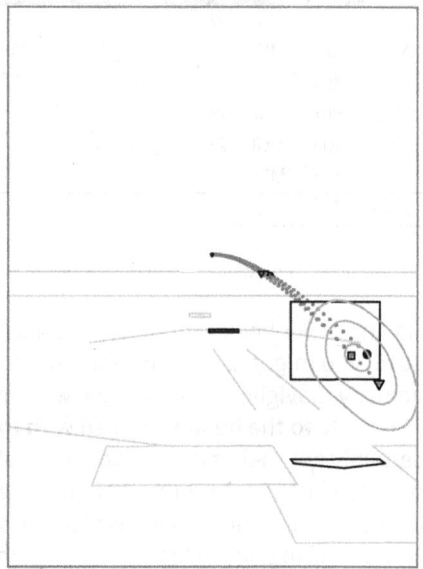

| Type | Frequency | Velocity | H Movement | V Movement |
|---|---|---|---|---|
| ● Fastball | 4.1% | 89.5 [92] | -10.5 [84] | -20.6 [88] |
| ◻ Sinker | 38.5% | 89.7 [85] | -12.2 [103] | -23.6 [89] |
| + Cutter | | | | |
| ▲ Changeup | 10.0% | 83 [92] | -11 [101] | -32.5 [85] |
| ✕ Splitter | | | | |
| ▽ Slider | 43.8% | 84.7 [101] | 0.8 [82] | -30.7 [107] |
| ◇ Curveball | 3.5% | 80.3 [106] | 4.5 [88] | -40.9 [114] |
| ✥ Slow Curveball | | | | |
| ✱ Knuckleball | | | | |
| ▼ Screwball | | | | |

## Ken Giles  RHP

Born: 09/20/90   Age: 29   Bats: R   Throws: R
Height: 6'3"   Weight: 210   Origin: Round 7, 2011 Draft (#241 overall)

| YEAR | TEAM | LVL | AGE | W | L | SV | G | GS | IP | H | HR | BB/9 | K/9 | K | GB% | BABIP |
|---|---|---|---|---|---|---|---|---|---|---|---|---|---|---|---|---|
| 2017 | HOU | MLB | 26 | 1 | 3 | 34 | 63 | 0 | 62² | 44 | 4 | 3.0 | 11.9 | 83 | 45% | .290 |
| 2018 | HOU | MLB | 27 | 0 | 2 | 12 | 34 | 0 | 30² | 36 | 2 | 0.9 | 9.1 | 31 | 37% | .366 |
| 2018 | TOR | MLB | 27 | 0 | 1 | 14 | 21 | 0 | 19² | 18 | 4 | 1.8 | 10.1 | 22 | 54% | .269 |
| 2019 | TOR | MLB | 28 | 2 | 3 | 23 | 53 | 0 | 53 | 36 | 5 | 2.9 | 14.1 | 83 | 39% | .301 |
| *2020* | *TOR* | *MLB* | *29* | *3* | *2* | *38* | *52* | *0* | *56* | *41* | *7* | *3.2* | *13.2* | *82* | *41%* | *.296* |

Comparables: Cody Allen, Greg Holland, Francisco Rodríguez

Timing is a funny thing. It took a particular set of circumstances, including a sustained stretch pronouncedly worse than the rest of his career, for Giles to land in Toronto. And it took different circumstances—the need for a cortisone shot in his pitching elbow just before the trade deadline that reportedly influenced the Yankees to back out of a trade—for the closer to complete a full season as an expat. Despite some brief layoffs, it was perhaps Giles' finest year, with the highest strikeout rate and lowest ERA of his career. A year from free agency, it's anyone's guess how the Jays use their best trade chip they actually intend to move—teams will be less bullish on one season of a volatile reliever than they would be on two.

| YEAR | TEAM | LVL | AGE | WHIP | ERA | DRA | WARP | MPH | FB% | WHF | CSP |
|---|---|---|---|---|---|---|---|---|---|---|---|
| 2017 | HOU | MLB | 26 | 1.04 | 2.30 | 2.85 | 1.6 | 100.1 | 52.8 | 17.2 | 49.1 |
| 2018 | HOU | MLB | 27 | 1.27 | 4.99 | 3.42 | 0.5 | 99.3 | 57.7 | 16.9 | 51.8 |
| 2018 | TOR | MLB | 27 | 1.12 | 4.12 | 3.18 | 0.4 | 99.1 | 61.3 | 16.3 | 48.9 |
| 2019 | TOR | MLB | 28 | 1.00 | 1.87 | 2.62 | 1.6 | 99.2 | 50.7 | 20.3 | 45.2 |
| *2020* | *TOR* | *MLB* | *29* | *1.10* | *2.81* | *3.03* | *1.3* | *98.8* | *53.9* | *18.3* | *48* |

# Toronto Blue Jays 2020

**Ken Giles, continued**

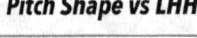
*Pitch Shape vs LHH*

*Pitch Shape vs RHH*

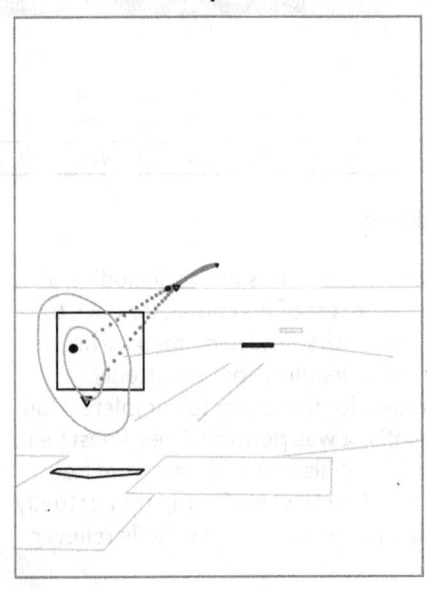

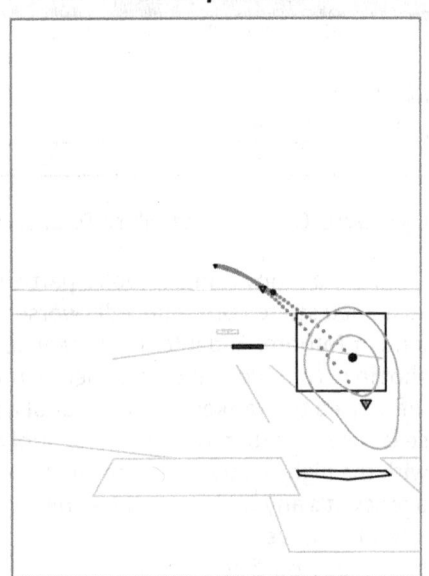

| Type | Frequency | Velocity | H Movement | V Movement |
|---|---|---|---|---|
| ● Fastball | 50.7% | 97.2 [114] | -8.6 [92] | -11.6 [111] |
| ☐ Sinker | | | | |
| + Cutter | | | | |
| ▲ Changeup | | | | |
| ✕ Splitter | | | | |
| ▽ Slider | 49.3% | 86.6 [109] | -0.6 [76] | -30 [109] |
| ◇ Curveball | | | | |
| ✦ Slow Curveball | | | | |
| ✱ Knuckleball | | | | |
| ▼ Screwball | | | | |

## Anthony Kay  LHP

Born: 03/21/95  Age: 25  Bats: L  Throws: L
Height: 6'0"  Weight: 218  Origin: Round 1, 2016 Draft (#31 overall)

| YEAR | TEAM | LVL | AGE | W | L | SV | G | GS | IP | H | HR | BB/9 | K/9 | K | GB% | BABIP |
|---|---|---|---|---|---|---|---|---|---|---|---|---|---|---|---|---|
| 2018 | COL | A | 23 | 4 | 4 | 0 | 13 | 13 | 69$^1$ | 73 | 6 | 2.9 | 10.1 | 78 | 45% | .356 |
| 2018 | SLU | A+ | 23 | 3 | 7 | 0 | 10 | 10 | 53$^1$ | 51 | 1 | 4.6 | 7.6 | 45 | 41% | .321 |
| 2019 | BIN | AA | 24 | 7 | 3 | 0 | 12 | 12 | 66$^1$ | 38 | 2 | 3.1 | 9.5 | 70 | 36% | .224 |
| 2019 | SYR | AAA | 24 | 1 | 3 | 0 | 7 | 7 | 31$^1$ | 40 | 7 | 3.2 | 7.5 | 26 | 33% | .355 |
| 2019 | BUF | AAA | 24 | 2 | 2 | 0 | 7 | 7 | 36 | 33 | 3 | 5.5 | 9.8 | 39 | 42% | .323 |
| 2019 | TOR | MLB | 24 | 1 | 0 | 0 | 3 | 2 | 14 | 15 | 0 | 3.2 | 8.4 | 13 | 55% | .341 |
| 2020 | TOR | MLB | 25 | 4 | 4 | 0 | 17 | 11 | 63 | 60 | 11 | 3.8 | 7.7 | 54 | 39% | .273 |

Comparables: Pedro Figueroa, Pat Light, Amir Garrett

According to Kay Jewelers, their "Every Kiss Begins With Kay" slogan was first used in 1985 and is now utilized in each of the company's commercials, giving them a 98 percent brand awareness rate. After being packaged from the Mets to the Blue Jays and making his major league debut in 2019, MLB's Kay cannot boast that kind of consciousness, but he's trending in the right direction. After his post-draft Tommy John surgery in 2016, Kay worked at five different minor league affiliates across the past two seasons before debuting for a three-game stint with Toronto. It's likely a back-of-the-rotation profile, but Kay has a clear pathway to starts in a rotation as barren and empty as Winterfell during Robb Stark's campaign through the Riverlands.

| YEAR | TEAM | LVL | AGE | WHIP | ERA | DRA | WARP | MPH | FB% | WHF | CSP |
|---|---|---|---|---|---|---|---|---|---|---|---|
| 2018 | COL | A | 23 | 1.37 | 4.54 | 5.46 | -0.2 | | | | |
| 2018 | SLU | A+ | 23 | 1.46 | 3.88 | 5.52 | -0.1 | | | | |
| 2019 | BIN | AA | 24 | 0.92 | 1.49 | 2.66 | 1.9 | | | | |
| 2019 | SYR | AAA | 24 | 1.63 | 6.61 | 5.87 | 0.3 | | | | |
| 2019 | BUF | AAA | 24 | 1.53 | 2.50 | 6.22 | 0.2 | | | | |
| 2019 | TOR | MLB | 24 | 1.43 | 5.79 | 4.76 | 0.1 | 95.4 | 61.6 | 12.4 | 45 |
| 2020 | TOR | MLB | 25 | 1.37 | 4.71 | 4.66 | 0.6 | 95.1 | 63.1 | 12.7 | 46.1 |

**Anthony Kay, continued**

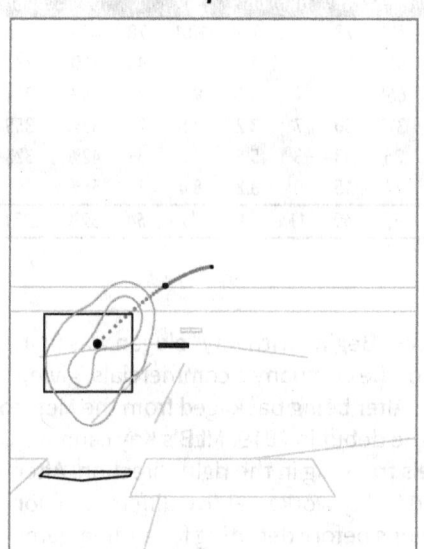
**Pitch Shape vs LHH**

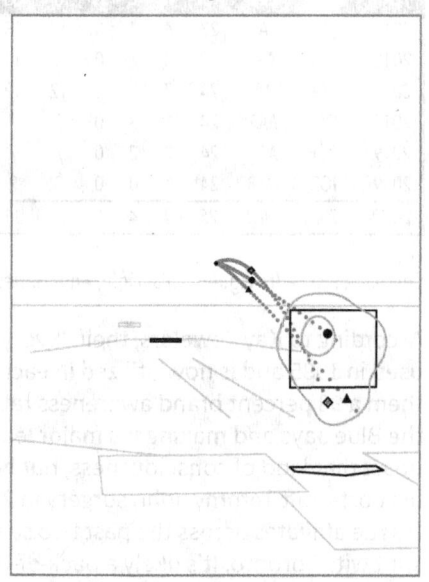
**Pitch Shape vs RHH**

| Type | Frequency | Velocity | H Movement | V Movement |
|---|---|---|---|---|
| ● Fastball | 61.2% | 93.8 [104] | 8.3 [94] | -13.7 [106] |
| ☐ Sinker | | | | |
| + Cutter | | | | |
| ▲ Changeup | 19.4% | 85.8 [102] | 14.4 [85] | -25.6 [105] |
| ✕ Splitter | | | | |
| ▽ Slider | | | | |
| ◇ Curveball | 19.0% | 78.4 [99] | -9 [106] | -46.7 [102] |
| ✦ Slow Curveball | | | | |
| ✱ Knuckleball | | | | |
| ▼ Screwball | | | | |

## Elvis Luciano   RHP

Born: 02/15/00   Age: 20   Bats: R   Throws: R
Height: 6'3"   Weight: 200   Origin: International Free Agent, 2016

| YEAR | TEAM | LVL | AGE | W | L | SV | G | GS | IP | H | HR | BB/9 | K/9 | K | GB% | BABIP |
|------|------|-----|-----|---|---|----|----|----|------|----|----|------|-----|----|-----|-------|
| 2017 | DDI | RK | 17 | 3 | 1 | 0 | 11 | 6 | 48$^1$ | 42 | 2 | 2.8 | 7.6 | 41 | 56% | .294 |
| 2017 | DIA | RK | 17 | 1 | 0 | 1 | 4 | 2 | 16$^1$ | 16 | 0 | 1.7 | 5.0 | 9 | 47% | .276 |
| 2018 | BNC | RK | 18 | 3 | 5 | 0 | 11 | 11 | 56 | 55 | 4 | 3.2 | 9.0 | 56 | 49% | .327 |
| 2018 | IDA | RK | 18 | 2 | 0 | 0 | 2 | 1 | 11 | 6 | 0 | 2.5 | 11.5 | 14 | 61% | .261 |
| 2019 | TOR | MLB | 19 | 1 | 0 | 0 | 25 | 0 | 33$^2$ | 36 | 4 | 6.4 | 7.2 | 27 | 38% | .317 |
| 2020 | TOR | MLB | 20 | 1 | 1 | 0 | 23 | 0 | 25 | 24 | 4 | 4.5 | 7.3 | 20 | 39% | .281 |

Comparables: Pedro Araujo, Felix Jorge, Brandon Maurer

Do you know where you were when the clock struck midnight on January 1, 2000? If so, you'll be bummed to learn that Luciano was not yet born, becoming the first pitcher born after Y2K to make the majors. Take heart, at least, that Luciano was rostered by the Blue Jays all season because of his status as a Rule 5 pick, and now the team has his rights he'll very likely spend all of 2020 in the minors. With experience, Luciano will attack hitters with more variation—he was almost exclusively fastball/slider against righties and fastball/change against lefties—and hopefully more strikes.

| YEAR | TEAM | LVL | AGE | WHIP | ERA | DRA | WARP | MPH | FB% | WHF | CSP |
|------|------|-----|-----|------|-----|-----|------|-----|-----|-----|-----|
| 2017 | DDI | RK | 17 | 1.18 | 2.98 | 3.47 | 1.2 | | | | |
| 2017 | DIA | RK | 17 | 1.16 | 2.76 | 3.58 | 0.4 | | | | |
| 2018 | BNC | RK | 18 | 1.34 | 4.66 | 4.11 | 1.2 | | | | |
| 2018 | IDA | RK | 18 | 0.82 | 0.00 | 1.82 | 0.5 | | | | |
| 2019 | TOR | MLB | 19 | 1.78 | 5.35 | 8.66 | -1.2 | 96.1 | 55.5 | 11.5 | 41.5 |
| 2020 | TOR | MLB | 20 | 1.48 | 5.19 | 5.05 | 0.0 | 96.5 | 58.5 | 12.1 | 43.8 |

# Toronto Blue Jays 2020

**Elvis Luciano, continued**

### Pitch Shape vs LHH

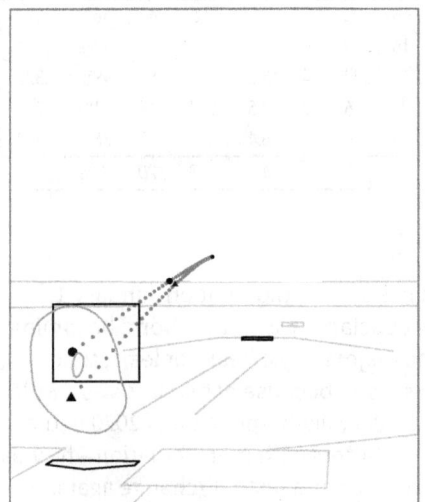

### Pitch Shape vs RHH

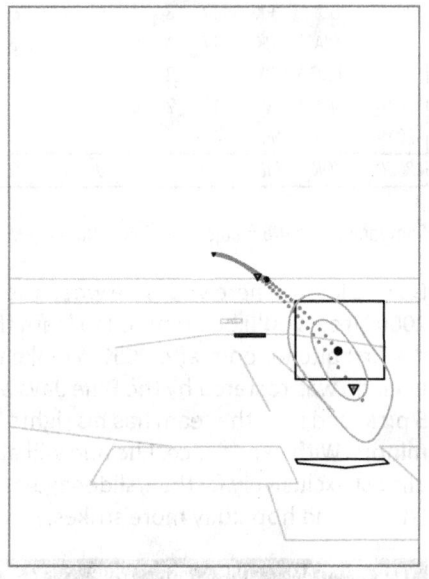

| Type | Frequency | Velocity | H Movement | V Movement |
|---|---|---|---|---|
| ● Fastball | 55.5% | 94.4 [106] | -12 [77] | -15 [102] |
| ☐ Sinker | | | | |
| + Cutter | | | | |
| ▲ Changeup | 19.2% | 88.1 [110] | -13.3 [90] | -27.4 [100] |
| ✕ Splitter | | | | |
| ▽ Slider | 25.3% | 84.7 [101] | 0.9 [83] | -32.5 [102] |
| ◇ Curveball | | | | |
| ✣ Slow Curveball | | | | |
| ✳ Knuckleball | | | | |
| ▼ Screwball | | | | |

## Tim Mayza   LHP

Born: 01/15/92   Age: 28   Bats: L   Throws: L
Height: 6'3"   Weight: 220   Origin: Round 12, 2013 Draft (#355 overall)

| YEAR | TEAM | LVL | AGE | W | L | SV | G | GS | IP | H | HR | BB/9 | K/9 | K | GB% | BABIP |
|---|---|---|---|---|---|---|---|---|---|---|---|---|---|---|---|---|
| 2017 | NHP | AA | 25 | 1 | 1 | 4 | 29 | 0 | 33$^1$ | 32 | 5 | 4.1 | 11.3 | 42 | 42% | .325 |
| 2017 | BUF | AAA | 25 | 1 | 1 | 0 | 11 | 0 | 19$^1$ | 16 | 0 | 3.3 | 7.4 | 16 | 33% | .276 |
| 2017 | TOR | MLB | 25 | 1 | 0 | 0 | 19 | 0 | 17 | 24 | 3 | 2.1 | 14.3 | 27 | 42% | .467 |
| 2018 | BUF | AAA | 26 | 6 | 2 | 1 | 20 | 0 | 25$^2$ | 26 | 2 | 3.9 | 12.6 | 36 | 42% | .400 |
| 2018 | TOR | MLB | 26 | 2 | 0 | 0 | 37 | 0 | 35$^2$ | 33 | 3 | 3.5 | 10.1 | 40 | 46% | .326 |
| 2019 | TOR | MLB | 27 | 1 | 3 | 0 | 68 | 0 | 51$^1$ | 45 | 8 | 4.7 | 9.6 | 55 | 53% | .272 |
| 2020 | TOR | MLB | 28 | 2 | 2 | 0 | 33 | 0 | 35 | 29 | 4 | 4.1 | 10.1 | 39 | 50% | .279 |

Comparables: Austin Davis, Emilio Pagán, Sam Freeman

Mayza suffered one of 2019's worst on-field injuries, falling to his knees on the mound and gripping his elbow after sailing a pitch behind Didi Gregorius. The southpaw will spend all of 2020 on the shelf and ultimately return to a league that will no longer tolerate his LOOGY inclinations—one-fourth of Mayza's team-high 68 appearances in 2019 were against two batters or fewer. Still, despite getting worse in each of his three big league seasons as his workload grew, Mayza was a slightly above-average reliever in 2019, per DRA-, and even in two years it's safe to say the Jays will be in need of decent arms.

| YEAR | TEAM | LVL | AGE | WHIP | ERA | DRA | WARP | MPH | FB% | WHF | CSP |
|---|---|---|---|---|---|---|---|---|---|---|---|
| 2017 | NHP | AA | 25 | 1.41 | 4.59 | 4.07 | 0.3 | | | | |
| 2017 | BUF | AAA | 25 | 1.19 | 0.93 | 3.72 | 0.3 | | | | |
| 2017 | TOR | MLB | 25 | 1.65 | 6.88 | 2.61 | 0.5 | 96.4 | 49.4 | 17.1 | 40.1 |
| 2018 | BUF | AAA | 26 | 1.44 | 4.56 | 4.49 | 0.2 | | | | |
| 2018 | TOR | MLB | 26 | 1.32 | 3.28 | 3.76 | 0.5 | 96.1 | 56 | 15.1 | 43.6 |
| 2019 | TOR | MLB | 27 | 1.40 | 4.91 | 4.68 | 0.4 | 96.1 | 64.5 | 15.6 | 38.6 |
| 2020 | TOR | MLB | 28 | 1.28 | 3.65 | 3.76 | 0.5 | 95.6 | 60.4 | 15.7 | 40.9 |

# Toronto Blue Jays 2020

*Tim Mayza, continued*

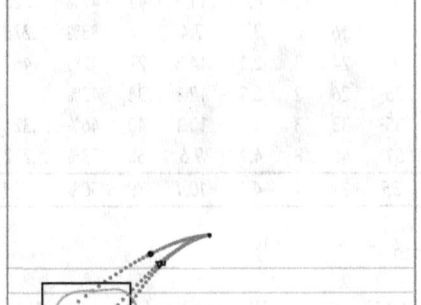
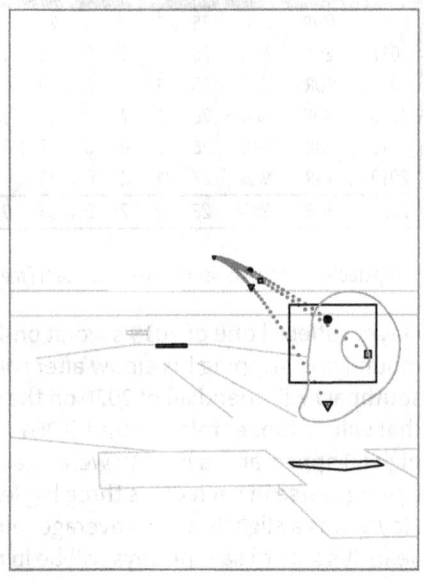

| Type | Frequency | Velocity | H Movement | V Movement |
|---|---|---|---|---|
| ● Fastball | 21.1% | 93.9 [104] | 8.7 [92] | -15.1 [102] |
| ☐ Sinker | 43.4% | 94.8 [111] | 14.5 [88] | -17.8 [109] |
| + Cutter | | | | |
| ▲ Changeup | | | | |
| ✕ Splitter | | | | |
| ▽ Slider | 35.4% | 88.1 [116] | 0.2 [78] | -28 [115] |
| ◇ Curveball | | | | |
| ✦ Slow Curveball | | | | |
| ✱ Knuckleball | | | | |
| ▼ Screwball | | | | |

## Brian Moran   LHP

Born: 09/30/88   Age: 31   Bats: L   Throws: L
Height: 6'4"   Weight: 230   Origin: Round 7, 2009 Draft (#203 overall)

| YEAR | TEAM | LVL | AGE | W | L | SV | G | GS | IP | H | HR | BB/9 | K/9 | K | GB% | BABIP |
|---|---|---|---|---|---|---|---|---|---|---|---|---|---|---|---|---|
| 2017 | TUL | AA | 28 | 0 | 1 | 1 | 19 | 0 | 19 | 12 | 1 | 1.4 | 12.8 | 27 | 38% | .282 |
| 2018 | TUL | AA | 29 | 1 | 1 | 3 | 22 | 0 | $26^2$ | 30 | 3 | 3.4 | 11.5 | 34 | 47% | .386 |
| 2018 | HFD | AA | 29 | 0 | 1 | 0 | 19 | 0 | $22^1$ | 15 | 1 | 2.8 | 12.9 | 32 | 44% | .286 |
| 2018 | OKL | AAA | 29 | 1 | 1 | 0 | 9 | 0 | $11^2$ | 16 | 0 | 3.9 | 7.7 | 10 | 42% | .390 |
| 2019 | NWO | AAA | 30 | 2 | 3 | 0 | 43 | 1 | 60 | 45 | 6 | 3.9 | 11.6 | 77 | 49% | .289 |
| 2019 | MIA | MLB | 30 | 1 | 0 | 0 | 10 | 0 | $6^1$ | 6 | 1 | 2.8 | 14.2 | 10 | 47% | .357 |
| 2020 | MIA | MLB | 31 | 1 | 1 | 0 | 11 | 0 | 12 | 10 | 3 | 3.4 | 7.9 | 10 | 41% | .248 |

Comparables: Bobby LaFromboise, Buddy Baumann, Pat Venditte

After ten years cutting his (now long) teeth in the minors, Moran debuted with the Marlins and immediately had to face his brother, the bearded Pirate Colin Moran, whom he promptly struck out. He's been a Rule 5 pick, a Tommy John recipient, a Mariner. He's been everywhere, man: Clinton, West Tenn, High Desert, Oklahoma / Jackson, Peoria, Pulaski and Tacoma / Bakersfield, Gwinnett, Caguas, Bridgeport / Hartford, Tulsa, New Orleans. The trials of this Sisyphean, down-and-out lefty pluck those country-western, literary, Crash Davis strings. Moran's hardships are those of many others, compounded but spread over many years, and his strong 2019 is evidence enough that baseball's chaos and ruthlessness can still accidentally produce some poetic justice.

| YEAR | TEAM | LVL | AGE | WHIP | ERA | DRA | WARP | MPH | FB% | WHF | CSP |
|---|---|---|---|---|---|---|---|---|---|---|---|
| 2017 | TUL | AA | 28 | 0.79 | 1.89 | 2.05 | 0.6 | | | | |
| 2018 | TUL | AA | 29 | 1.50 | 3.71 | 4.71 | 0.1 | | | | |
| 2018 | HFD | AA | 29 | 0.99 | 2.42 | 2.38 | 0.7 | | | | |
| 2018 | OKL | AAA | 29 | 1.80 | 6.17 | 6.31 | -0.2 | | | | |
| 2019 | NWO | AAA | 30 | 1.18 | 3.15 | 2.65 | 2.1 | | | | |
| 2019 | MIA | MLB | 30 | 1.26 | 4.26 | 3.82 | 0.1 | 86.3 | 56.3 | 14.3 | 48.7 |
| 2020 | MIA | MLB | 31 | 1.28 | 4.62 | 4.97 | 0.1 | 85.5 | 55.9 | 14.2 | 48.5 |

# Toronto Blue Jays 2020

**Brian Moran, continued**

### Pitch Shape vs LHH

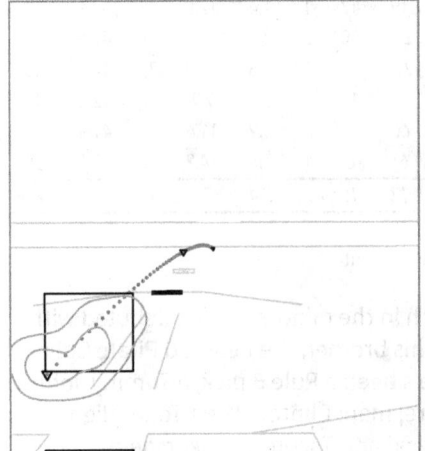

### Pitch Shape vs RHH

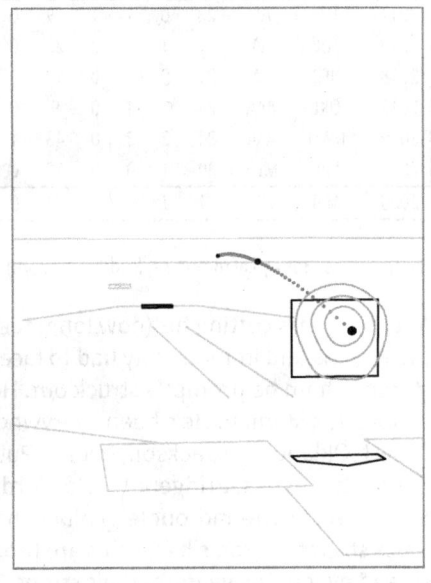

| Type | Frequency | Velocity | H Movement | V Movement |
|---|---|---|---|---|
| ● Fastball | 52.7% | 84.7 [78] | 1.1 [126] | -25.4 [75] |
| □ Sinker | 3.6% | 85.3 [62] | 7.8 [131] | -25.8 [81] |
| + Cutter | | | | |
| ▲ Changeup | | | | |
| ✕ Splitter | | | | |
| ▽ Slider | 43.8% | 72.3 [49] | -17.8 [153] | -44.9 [66] |
| ◇ Curveball | | | | |
| ⊕ Slow Curveball | | | | |
| ✱ Knuckleball | | | | |
| ▼ Screwball | | | | |

## Thomas Pannone LHP

Born: 04/28/94 Age: 26 Bats: L Throws: L
Height: 6'0" Weight: 200 Origin: Round 9, 2013 Draft (#261 overall)

| YEAR | TEAM | LVL | AGE | W | L | SV | G | GS | IP | H | HR | BB/9 | K/9 | K | GB% | BABIP |
|---|---|---|---|---|---|---|---|---|---|---|---|---|---|---|---|---|
| 2017 | LYN | A+ | 23 | 2 | 0 | 0 | 5 | 5 | 27² | 10 | 0 | 2.3 | 12.7 | 39 | 48% | .212 |
| 2017 | AKR | AA | 23 | 6 | 1 | 0 | 14 | 14 | 82¹ | 67 | 5 | 2.3 | 8.9 | 81 | 37% | .281 |
| 2017 | NHP | AA | 23 | 1 | 2 | 0 | 6 | 6 | 34² | 31 | 9 | 2.1 | 7.5 | 29 | 38% | .232 |
| 2018 | NHP | AA | 24 | 0 | 0 | 0 | 2 | 2 | 9 | 9 | 1 | 5.0 | 12.0 | 12 | 29% | .348 |
| 2018 | BUF | AAA | 24 | 0 | 3 | 0 | 6 | 6 | 36² | 40 | 8 | 1.7 | 9.8 | 40 | 24% | .327 |
| 2018 | TOR | MLB | 24 | 4 | 1 | 0 | 12 | 6 | 43 | 37 | 7 | 3.1 | 6.1 | 29 | 36% | .234 |
| 2019 | BUF | AAA | 25 | 3 | 1 | 0 | 8 | 6 | 33² | 25 | 4 | 4.0 | 11.0 | 41 | 34% | .262 |
| 2019 | TOR | MLB | 25 | 3 | 6 | 0 | 37 | 7 | 73 | 73 | 13 | 3.8 | 8.5 | 69 | 35% | .291 |
| 2020 | TOR | MLB | 26 | 2 | 2 | 0 | 41 | 0 | 43 | 45 | 10 | 3.6 | 8.1 | 39 | 35% | .286 |

Comparables: Jalen Beeks, Jharel Cotton, Tyler Wilson

Jumbo shrimp, spend'n'save, Pannone. All oxymorons, the prior trio each contain their opposites, presenting intriguing contradictions. Pannone lived up to his surname with his 2019 season a bevy of contradictions. In seven starts he took five losses and compiled an 11.54 ERA. In 30 relief appearances his ERA was 3.54. Less self-contradictory is Pannone's profile, and while the stark contrast between his success in Triple-A and his struggles in the majors present a conundrum, it's one we've all seen before, and one Pannone will need to overcome to dial his usage from 'none' to 'pan.'

| YEAR | TEAM | LVL | AGE | WHIP | ERA | DRA | WARP | MPH | FB% | WHF | CSP |
|---|---|---|---|---|---|---|---|---|---|---|---|
| 2017 | LYN | A+ | 23 | 0.61 | 0.00 | 1.77 | 1.1 | | | | |
| 2017 | AKR | AA | 23 | 1.07 | 2.62 | 4.05 | 1.1 | | | | |
| 2017 | NHP | AA | 23 | 1.12 | 3.63 | 5.27 | 0.0 | | | | |
| 2018 | NHP | AA | 24 | 1.56 | 3.00 | 4.32 | 0.1 | | | | |
| 2018 | BUF | AAA | 24 | 1.28 | 4.91 | 5.49 | 0.0 | | | | |
| 2018 | TOR | MLB | 24 | 1.21 | 4.19 | 5.89 | -0.3 | 90.4 | 64.2 | 10.4 | 50.6 |
| 2019 | BUF | AAA | 25 | 1.19 | 3.21 | 2.96 | 1.2 | | | | |
| 2019 | TOR | MLB | 25 | 1.42 | 6.16 | 6.48 | -0.8 | 92.3 | 61.7 | 11.9 | 46.2 |
| 2020 | TOR | MLB | 26 | 1.44 | 5.51 | 5.31 | -0.1 | 91.3 | 63.6 | 11.6 | 49 |

# Toronto Blue Jays 2020

**Thomas Pannone, continued**

### Pitch Shape vs LHH

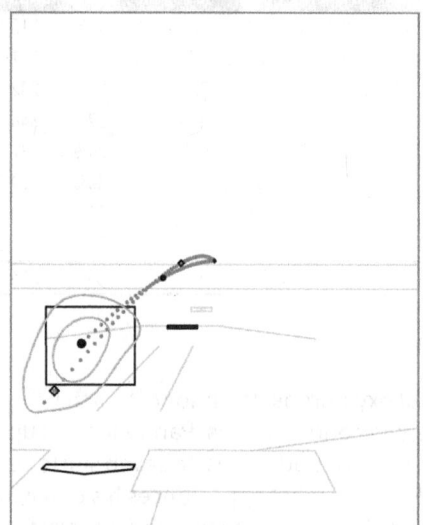

### Pitch Shape vs RHH

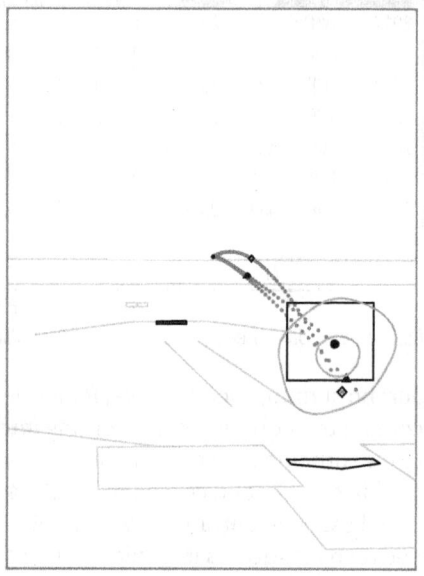

| Type | Frequency | Velocity | H Movement | V Movement |
|---|---|---|---|---|
| ● Fastball | 61.7% | 90.1 [93] | 10.8 [83] | -16.3 [99] |
| ☐ Sinker | | | | |
| + Cutter | | | | |
| ▲ Changeup | 15.4% | 83.7 [94] | 14.3 [85] | -27.9 [99] |
| ✕ Splitter | | | | |
| ▽ Slider | | | | |
| ◇ Curveball | 22.9% | 74 [85] | -11.7 [117] | -50.5 [94] |
| ⊕ Slow Curveball | | | | |
| ✱ Knuckleball | | | | |
| ▼ Screwball | | | | |

## Sean Reid-Foley  RHP

Born: 08/30/95  Age: 24  Bats: R  Throws: R
Height: 6'3"  Weight: 220  Origin: Round 2, 2014 Draft (#49 overall)

| YEAR | TEAM | LVL | AGE | W | L | SV | G | GS | IP | H | HR | BB/9 | K/9 | K | GB% | BABIP |
|---|---|---|---|---|---|---|---|---|---|---|---|---|---|---|---|---|
| 2017 | NHP | AA | 21 | 10 | 11 | 0 | 27 | 27 | 132$^2$ | 145 | 22 | 3.6 | 8.3 | 122 | 42% | .318 |
| 2018 | NHP | AA | 22 | 5 | 0 | 0 | 8 | 8 | 44$^1$ | 27 | 3 | 4.1 | 10.6 | 52 | 55% | .240 |
| 2018 | BUF | AAA | 22 | 7 | 5 | 0 | 16 | 16 | 85$^1$ | 76 | 5 | 3.2 | 10.3 | 98 | 43% | .318 |
| 2018 | TOR | MLB | 22 | 2 | 4 | 0 | 7 | 7 | 33$^1$ | 31 | 6 | 5.7 | 11.3 | 42 | 36% | .312 |
| 2019 | BUF | AAA | 23 | 3 | 5 | 0 | 20 | 19 | 89 | 78 | 13 | 6.6 | 10.6 | 105 | 44% | .293 |
| 2019 | TOR | MLB | 23 | 2 | 4 | 0 | 9 | 6 | 31$^2$ | 33 | 5 | 6.0 | 8.0 | 28 | 42% | .298 |
| 2020 | TOR | MLB | 24 | 2 | 2 | 0 | 41 | 0 | 43 | 42 | 8 | 5.2 | 8.9 | 43 | 42% | .294 |

Comparables: Touki Toussaint, Zack Littell, Robert Stephenson

On August 14th, history was made as Reid-Foley pitched to the Rangers' Isiah Kiner-Falefa, creating MLB's first-ever pitcher-hitter matchup with two hyphenated last names. For those in the know, the factoid sparked a debate over whether this first was interesting-boring, or whether it was bad-worse. Entering the season as the Jays' seventh-ranked prospect, Reid-Foley's issues with command only intensified; he walked at least six per nine in both Triple-A and Toronto. Even more concerning, the 24-year-old's fastball dipped more than a full tick—things were so grim that the Blue Jays seemed perfectly justified not calling up Reid-Foley in September. At this point, Reid-Foley's development is clearly off-track, and there's little in his career to show that the command issues are a blip.

| YEAR | TEAM | LVL | AGE | WHIP | ERA | DRA | WARP | MPH | FB% | WHF | CSP |
|---|---|---|---|---|---|---|---|---|---|---|---|
| 2017 | NHP | AA | 21 | 1.49 | 5.09 | 5.50 | -0.5 | | | | |
| 2018 | NHP | AA | 22 | 1.06 | 2.03 | 2.66 | 1.4 | | | | |
| 2018 | BUF | AAA | 22 | 1.24 | 3.90 | 4.06 | 1.4 | | | | |
| 2018 | TOR | MLB | 22 | 1.56 | 5.13 | 4.95 | 0.1 | 95.9 | 63.2 | 13.1 | 47.3 |
| 2019 | BUF | AAA | 23 | 1.61 | 6.47 | 4.95 | 1.5 | | | | |
| 2019 | TOR | MLB | 23 | 1.71 | 4.26 | 7.57 | -0.6 | 95.1 | 50.2 | 11.2 | 46.2 |
| 2020 | TOR | MLB | 24 | 1.56 | 5.52 | 5.20 | 0.0 | 95.3 | 57.8 | 12.4 | 48.1 |

# Toronto Blue Jays 2020

**Sean Reid-Foley, continued**

### Pitch Shape vs LHH

### Pitch Shape vs RHH

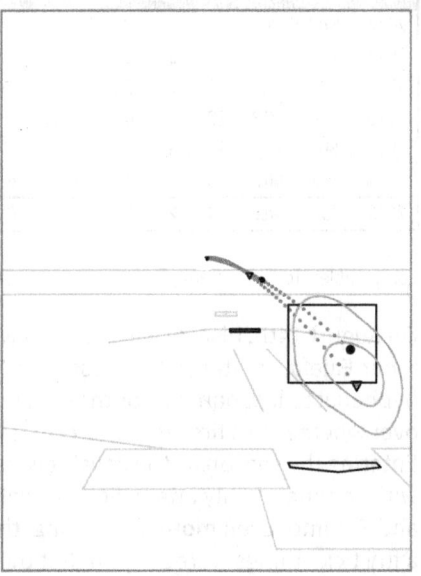

| Type | Frequency | Velocity | H Movement | V Movement |
|---|---|---|---|---|
| ● Fastball | 48.0% | 93 [102] | -7.9 [95] | -14.9 [103] |
| ☐ Sinker | | | | |
| + Cutter | | | | |
| ▲ Changeup | 8.7% | 86.2 [103] | -12.4 [94] | -27.2 [100] |
| ✕ Splitter | | | | |
| ▽ Slider | 34.4% | 84.1 [99] | 4.7 [99] | -32.8 [101] |
| ◇ Curveball | 6.7% | 81.3 [109] | 11.4 [116] | -42.5 [111] |
| ✦ Slow Curveball | | | | |
| ✳ Knuckleball | | | | |
| ▼ Screwball | | | | |

## Tanner Roark  RHP

Born: 10/05/86  Age: 33  Bats: R  Throws: R
Height: 6'2"  Weight: 240  Origin: Round 25, 2008 Draft (#753 overall)

| YEAR | TEAM | LVL | AGE | W | L | SV | G | GS | IP | H | HR | BB/9 | K/9 | K | GB% | BABIP |
|---|---|---|---|---|---|---|---|---|---|---|---|---|---|---|---|---|
| 2017 | WAS | MLB | 30 | 13 | 11 | 0 | 32 | 30 | 181[1] | 178 | 23 | 3.2 | 8.2 | 166 | 49% | .300 |
| 2018 | WAS | MLB | 31 | 9 | 15 | 0 | 31 | 30 | 180[1] | 181 | 24 | 2.5 | 7.3 | 146 | 43% | .296 |
| 2019 | CIN | MLB | 32 | 6 | 7 | 0 | 21 | 21 | 110[1] | 119 | 14 | 3.1 | 8.8 | 108 | 38% | .333 |
| 2019 | OAK | MLB | 32 | 4 | 3 | 0 | 10 | 10 | 55 | 61 | 14 | 2.1 | 8.2 | 50 | 35% | .301 |
| 2020 | TOR | MLB | 33 | 8 | 7 | 0 | 28 | 28 | 119 | 119 | 20 | 2.8 | 8.1 | 107 | 38% | .291 |

Comparables: Andrew Cashner, Daniel Hudson, Matt Shoemaker

Roark's numbers generally vacillate based on how well he suppresses homers. When the baseballs were normal in the early part of his career, Roark shined. In subsequent years, as hitters have benefited from a ball increasingly composed of the active ingredients in Silly Putty, his HR/FB rate soared and his performance commensurately dipped. Taken together, Roark's history as a strike-thrower capable of eating innings suggests he'll have his uses going forward. But free agency just isn't what it used to be, especially for sorta-athletic 33-year-old pitchers without a manifestly compelling explanation for his middling performance. Therefore, it was a pleasant surprise to see Roark get a two-year contract from the Blue Jays worth $24 million.

| YEAR | TEAM | LVL | AGE | WHIP | ERA | DRA | WARP | MPH | FB% | WHF | CSP |
|---|---|---|---|---|---|---|---|---|---|---|---|
| 2017 | WAS | MLB | 30 | 1.33 | 4.67 | 3.89 | 3.4 | 94.6 | 56.2 | 10.7 | 45.3 |
| 2018 | WAS | MLB | 31 | 1.28 | 4.34 | 4.89 | 0.9 | 93.5 | 59.2 | 9.2 | 46.9 |
| 2019 | CIN | MLB | 32 | 1.42 | 4.24 | 5.27 | 0.6 | 94.3 | 61 | 9.9 | 44.9 |
| 2019 | OAK | MLB | 32 | 1.35 | 4.58 | 6.73 | -0.6 | 93.7 | 61 | 9.5 | 48.7 |
| 2020 | TOR | MLB | 33 | 1.31 | 4.52 | 4.53 | 1.4 | 93.0 | 58.4 | 9.7 | 45.7 |

# Toronto Blue Jays 2020

**Tanner Roark, continued**

**Pitch Shape vs LHH**

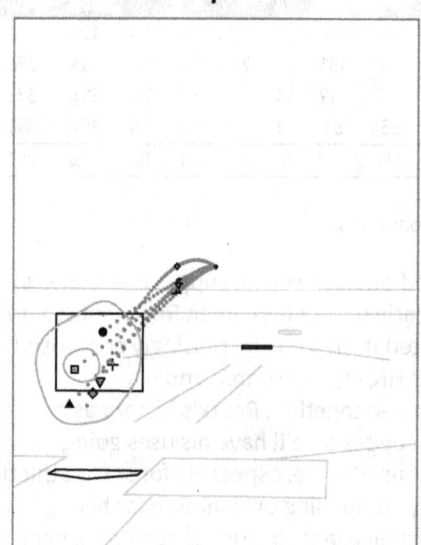

**Pitch Shape vs RHH**

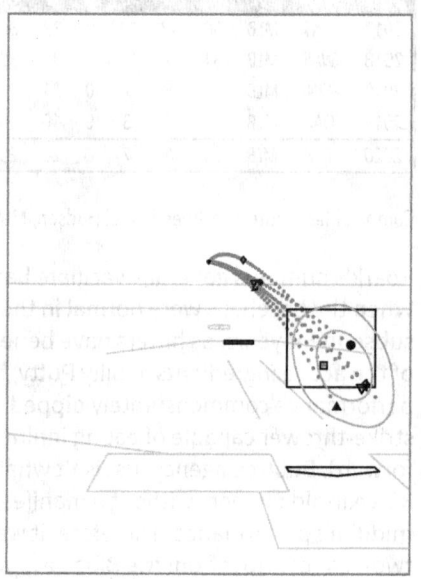

| Type | Frequency | Velocity | H Movement | V Movement |
|---|---|---|---|---|
| ● Fastball | 24.9% | 92.4 [100] | -4 [113] | -13.2 [107] |
| □ Sinker | 30.4% | 92.2 [98] | -11.1 [110] | -16.2 [115] |
| + Cutter | 4.5% | 88.2 [97] | 2.4 [104] | -23.3 [103] |
| ▲ Changeup | 9.9% | 84.4 [97] | -11 [101] | -25.1 [107] |
| ✕ Splitter | | | | |
| ▽ Slider | 17.5% | 86.2 [108] | 3.3 [93] | -27.5 [116] |
| ◇ Curveball | 12.9% | 76 [91] | 11.3 [115] | -55.6 [83] |
| ◆ Slow Curveball | | | | |
| ✷ Knuckleball | | | | |
| ▼ Screwball | | | | |

## Jordan Romano  RHP

Born: 04/21/93  Age: 27  Bats: R  Throws: R
Height: 6'4"  Weight: 200  Origin: Round 10, 2014 Draft (#294 overall)

| YEAR | TEAM | LVL | AGE | W | L | SV | G | GS | IP | H | HR | BB/9 | K/9 | K | GB% | BABIP |
|---|---|---|---|---|---|---|---|---|---|---|---|---|---|---|---|---|
| 2017 | DUN | A+ | 24 | 7 | 5 | 0 | 28 | 26 | 138 | 141 | 2 | 3.5 | 9.0 | 138 | 38% | .344 |
| 2018 | NHP | AA | 25 | 11 | 8 | 0 | 25 | 25 | 137$^1$ | 122 | 15 | 2.7 | 8.2 | 125 | 38% | .279 |
| 2019 | BUF | AAA | 26 | 2 | 2 | 5 | 24 | 3 | 37$^2$ | 37 | 8 | 3.3 | 12.7 | 53 | 40% | .333 |
| 2019 | TOR | MLB | 26 | 0 | 2 | 0 | 17 | 0 | 15$^1$ | 17 | 4 | 5.3 | 12.3 | 21 | 51% | .351 |
| 2020 | TOR | MLB | 27 | 2 | 2 | 0 | 35 | 0 | 37 | 32 | 7 | 4.0 | 9.8 | 40 | 40% | .274 |

Comparables: Seth Lugo, Phillips Valdez, Mike Bolsinger

Selected in the Rule 5 Draft last winter and passing from the White Sox to Rangers before being returned after failing to scratch the Texas bullpen, Romano hit the bigs anyways in 2019. Finally completing a long-expected move to the bullpen, the flamethrower gave a number of reasons for confidence in the choice. The ERA was rough, both in Triple-A and his three stints as a Blue Jay, but bushels of strikeouts and grounders give fans license to dream on improvement. Romano may just be a two-pitch reliever at this point, but with a biting slider that can get whiffs against both righties and lefties, Romano has as good a chance as anyone to emerge as the heir to Ken Giles in the Great White North.

| YEAR | TEAM | LVL | AGE | WHIP | ERA | DRA | WARP | MPH | FB% | WHF | CSP |
|---|---|---|---|---|---|---|---|---|---|---|---|
| 2017 | DUN | A+ | 24 | 1.41 | 3.39 | 5.30 | -0.1 | | | | |
| 2018 | NHP | AA | 25 | 1.19 | 4.13 | 3.82 | 2.4 | | | | |
| 2019 | BUF | AAA | 26 | 1.35 | 5.73 | 4.27 | 0.8 | | | | |
| 2019 | TOR | MLB | 26 | 1.70 | 7.63 | 4.07 | 0.2 | 97.2 | 63.7 | 14.1 | 45.8 |
| 2020 | TOR | MLB | 27 | 1.32 | 4.45 | 4.42 | 0.3 | 96.7 | 64.4 | 14.3 | 46.3 |

# Toronto Blue Jays 2020

**Jordan Romano, continued**

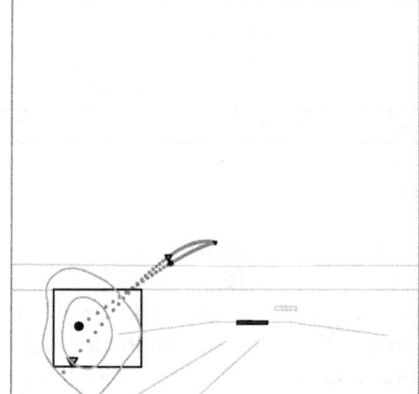
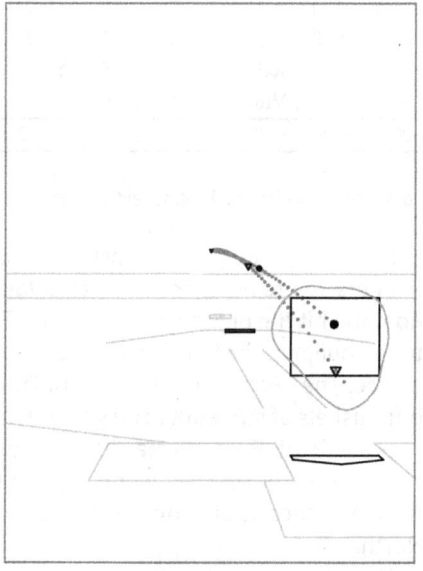

| Type | Frequency | Velocity | H Movement | V Movement |
|---|---|---|---|---|
| ● Fastball | 63.7% | 95 [108] | -5.9 [104] | -13 [108] |
| ☐ Sinker | | | | |
| + Cutter | | | | |
| ▲ Changeup | | | | |
| ✕ Splitter | | | | |
| ▽ Slider | 36.3% | 85.1 [103] | 3.7 [94] | -35.5 [93] |
| ◇ Curveball | | | | |
| ⬥ Slow Curveball | | | | |
| ✳ Knuckleball | | | | |
| ▼ Screwball | | | | |

## Hyun-Jin Ryu  LHP

Born: 03/25/87  Age: 33  Bats: R  Throws: L
Height: 6'3"  Weight: 255  Origin: International Free Agent, 2013

| YEAR | TEAM | LVL | AGE | W | L | SV | G | GS | IP | H | HR | BB/9 | K/9 | K | GB% | BABIP |
|---|---|---|---|---|---|---|---|---|---|---|---|---|---|---|---|---|
| 2017 | LAN | MLB | 30 | 5 | 9 | 1 | 25 | 24 | 126$^2$ | 128 | 22 | 3.2 | 8.2 | 116 | 48% | .299 |
| 2018 | LAN | MLB | 31 | 7 | 3 | 0 | 15 | 15 | 82$^1$ | 68 | 9 | 1.6 | 9.7 | 89 | 47% | .281 |
| 2019 | LAN | MLB | 32 | 14 | 5 | 0 | 29 | 29 | 182$^2$ | 160 | 17 | 1.2 | 8.0 | 163 | 53% | .280 |
| 2020 | TOR | MLB | 33 | 10 | 7 | 0 | 26 | 26 | 143 | 132 | 20 | 1.9 | 8.3 | 131 | 51% | .281 |

Comparables: Kris Medlen, Shane Reynolds, Ron Guidry

It's a wonder that Ryu is even pitching. Labrum tears have felled better pitchers than him, and Ryu's rehabilitation was complicated by an additional elbow surgery. Following a near two-year absence, the lefty re-established himself as an effective starter in 2017, found another gear in 2018, and authored a Cy-worthy season last year. Ryu wrote in black ink, too, leading the league in ERA and walks-per-nine, across 29 starts. A late-season swoon that saw him relent to the year of the homer paired with some "load management" from the Dodgers to ultimately sink his chances to take home the hardware.

Ryu accepted the qualifying offer last offseason, taking a chance on himself and his health. He won that gamble and headed into free agency looking for a more significant guarantee in both years and dollars. Despite what must have been a close eye on MRIs of his shoulder and groin, he got just that by signing a four-year deal with the Blue Jays worth $80 million. The underlying peripherals that say he's more of a fringe frontline arm than the ace he was in 2019, but the story of his climb back up the mountain is an inspiration.

| YEAR | TEAM | LVL | AGE | WHIP | ERA | DRA | WARP | MPH | FB% | WHF | CSP |
|---|---|---|---|---|---|---|---|---|---|---|---|
| 2017 | LAN | MLB | 30 | 1.37 | 3.77 | 4.18 | 2.0 | 92.6 | 36.8 | 11.4 | 41 |
| 2018 | LAN | MLB | 31 | 1.01 | 1.97 | 2.45 | 2.7 | 92.4 | 37 | 12.6 | 49.8 |
| 2019 | LAN | MLB | 32 | 1.01 | 2.32 | 3.03 | 5.4 | 92.5 | 40.6 | 12.4 | 47.5 |
| 2020 | TOR | MLB | 33 | 1.14 | 3.39 | 3.60 | 3.1 | 91.5 | 38.4 | 12 | 46.1 |

# Toronto Blue Jays 2020

**Hyun-Jin Ryu, continued**

**Pitch Shape vs LHH**

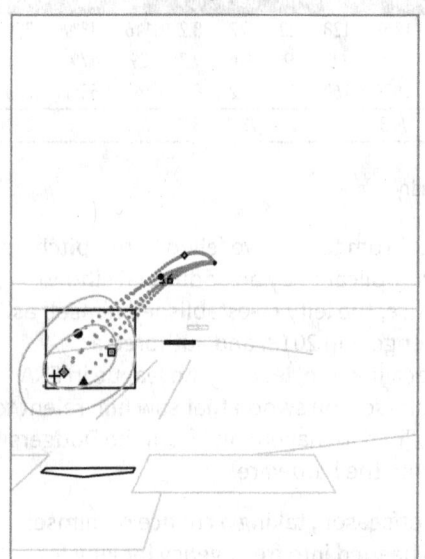

**Pitch Shape vs RHH**

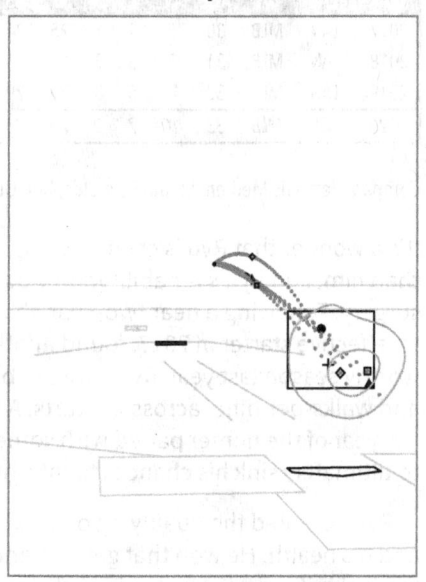

| Type | Frequency | Velocity | H Movement | V Movement |
|---|---|---|---|---|
| ● Fastball | 26.3% | 91 [96] | 9.4 [89] | -17.4 [96] |
| □ Sinker | 14.2% | 90.4 [89] | 14.2 [90] | -22 [94] |
| + Cutter | 19.4% | 87.2 [91] | -0.6 [93] | -25.4 [95] |
| ▲ Changeup | 27.4% | 80.3 [82] | 11.8 [97] | -33 [84] |
| ✕ Splitter | | | | |
| ▽ Slider | | | | |
| ◇ Curveball | 12.1% | 72.9 [81] | -11.2 [115] | -58.4 [77] |
| ◈ Slow Curveball | | | | |
| ✳ Knuckleball | | | | |
| ▼ Screwball | | | | |

## Matt Shoemaker  RHP

Born: 09/27/86   Age: 33   Bats: R   Throws: R
Height: 6'2"   Weight: 225   Origin: Undrafted Free Agent, 2008

| YEAR | TEAM | LVL | AGE | W | L | SV | G | GS | IP | H | HR | BB/9 | K/9 | K | GB% | BABIP |
|---|---|---|---|---|---|---|---|---|---|---|---|---|---|---|---|---|
| 2017 | LAA | MLB | 30 | 6 | 3 | 0 | 14 | 14 | 77² | 73 | 15 | 3.2 | 8.0 | 69 | 40% | .278 |
| 2018 | LAA | MLB | 31 | 2 | 2 | 0 | 7 | 7 | 31 | 29 | 3 | 2.9 | 9.6 | 33 | 44% | .313 |
| 2019 | TOR | MLB | 32 | 3 | 0 | 0 | 5 | 5 | 28² | 16 | 3 | 2.8 | 7.5 | 24 | 51% | .183 |
| 2020 | TOR | MLB | 33 | 5 | 4 | 0 | 15 | 15 | 80 | 78 | 14 | 3.2 | 9.0 | 80 | 43% | .292 |

Comparables: Tanner Roark, Collin McHugh, Chris Rusin

Through the first four starts of Shoemaker's first run with a team based outside of Anaheim (and the United States), it seemed that he was back to the form that made him a valuable back-of-the-rotation piece for the Angels—or better, given the 1.75 ERA he entered start number five with. That one only lasted three (scoreless) frames, however, before Shoemaker suffered a nasty and demoralizing knee injury: a torn ACL that ended his seventh year and contributed to the 21 starters Toronto used in 2019. After three consecutive years throwing at least 135 innings with above-average DRAs, Shoemaker has had a more bedraggled trio of campaigns than, well, an oft-cobbled shoe. Entering his last year of arbitration eligibility, the 33-year-old will need to break this streak of injury-shortened seasons at three to find a guaranteed deal in free agency.

| YEAR | TEAM | LVL | AGE | WHIP | ERA | DRA | WARP | MPH | FB% | WHF | CSP |
|---|---|---|---|---|---|---|---|---|---|---|---|
| 2017 | LAA | MLB | 30 | 1.30 | 4.52 | 5.86 | -0.2 | 94.4 | 49.5 | 12.4 | 45.6 |
| 2018 | LAA | MLB | 31 | 1.26 | 4.94 | 5.60 | -0.1 | 94.1 | 47.1 | 13.4 | 46.2 |
| 2019 | TOR | MLB | 32 | 0.87 | 1.57 | 4.57 | 0.4 | 93.2 | 46.7 | 13.9 | 40.9 |
| 2020 | TOR | MLB | 33 | 1.33 | 4.60 | 4.58 | 0.9 | 92.9 | 47.6 | 12.9 | 43.3 |

# Toronto Blue Jays 2020

*Matt Shoemaker, continued*

**Pitch Shape vs LHH**          **Pitch Shape vs RHH**

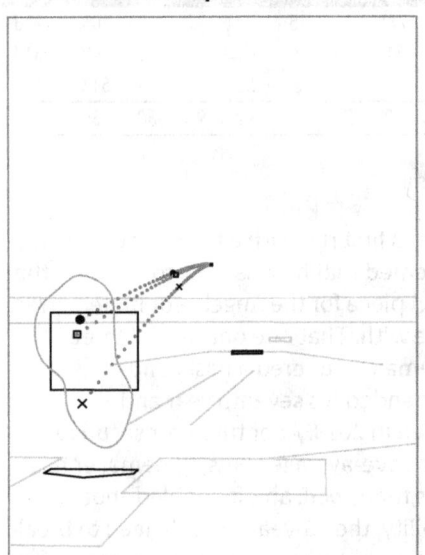 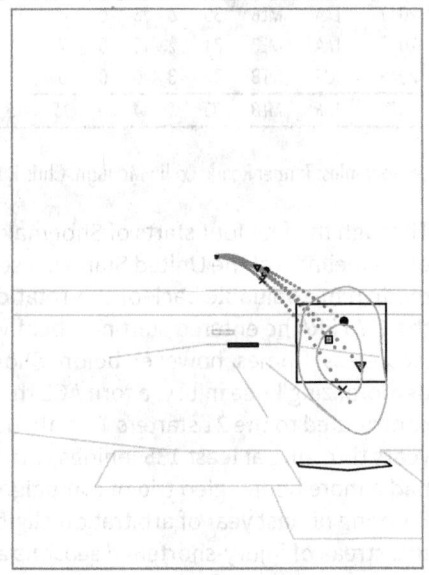

| Type | Frequency | Velocity | H Movement | V Movement |
|---|---|---|---|---|
| ● Fastball | 17.9% | 90.8 [96] | -8 [95] | -14.9 [103] |
| ☐ Sinker | 28.7% | 91 [92] | -13.9 [92] | -19.1 [105] |
| + Cutter | | | | |
| ▲ Changeup | | | | |
| ✕ Splitter | 33.3% | 84.9 [99] | -10.2 [92] | -29.4 [99] |
| ▽ Slider | 17.7% | 82.1 [90] | 2 [88] | -33.8 [98] |
| ◇ Curveball | | | | |
| ⊕ Slow Curveball | | | | |
| ✳ Knuckleball | | | | |
| ▼ Screwball | | | | |

## Trent Thornton  RHP

Born: 09/30/93  Age: 26  Bats: R  Throws: R
Height: 6'0"  Weight: 195  Origin: Round 5, 2015 Draft (#139 overall)

| YEAR | TEAM | LVL | AGE | W | L | SV | G | GS | IP | H | HR | BB/9 | K/9 | K | GB% | BABIP |
|---|---|---|---|---|---|---|---|---|---|---|---|---|---|---|---|---|
| 2017 | CCH | AA | 23 | 1 | 2 | 0 | 4 | 3 | 16$^1$ | 25 | 2 | 0.0 | 7.2 | 13 | 57% | .377 |
| 2017 | FRE | AAA | 23 | 8 | 4 | 0 | 21 | 20 | 115 | 137 | 12 | 1.8 | 6.9 | 88 | 47% | .338 |
| 2018 | FRE | AAA | 24 | 9 | 8 | 0 | 24 | 22 | 124$^1$ | 118 | 13 | 2.2 | 8.8 | 122 | 42% | .304 |
| 2019 | TOR | MLB | 25 | 6 | 9 | 0 | 32 | 29 | 154$^1$ | 156 | 24 | 3.6 | 8.7 | 149 | 34% | .301 |
| 2020 | TOR | MLB | 26 | 6 | 5 | 0 | 32 | 15 | 91 | 90 | 16 | 3.6 | 8.5 | 87 | 35% | .292 |

Comparables: Andrew Moore, P.J. Walters, John Gant

Thornton, the 2018 Arizona Fall League roommate of Forrest Whitley before being dealt to Toronto, had a subsequent season in many ways on the opposite end of the spectrum from the top prospect. For one, Thornton not only debuted with Toronto but spent the entire season in the bigs and the rotation, leading the team in both starts and innings. The results were middling, but likely enough to earn the UNC product a spot this year in Toronto's depleted rotation. He also had the winter to continue working on the changeup and curve grips Clay Buchholz helped him develop. But ultimately, the biggest difference between the two former roommates is that Thornton is the kind of placeholder that gets moved aside when a prospect like Whitley is ready. Fortunately for the 25-year-old sophomore, that doesn't appear to be an imminent concern in this organization.

| YEAR | TEAM | LVL | AGE | WHIP | ERA | DRA | WARP | MPH | FB% | WHF | CSP |
|---|---|---|---|---|---|---|---|---|---|---|---|
| 2017 | CCH | AA | 23 | 1.53 | 6.06 | 6.37 | -0.3 | | | | |
| 2017 | FRE | AAA | 23 | 1.39 | 5.09 | 5.02 | 0.8 | | | | |
| 2018 | FRE | AAA | 24 | 1.20 | 4.42 | 4.08 | 2.0 | | | | |
| 2019 | TOR | MLB | 25 | 1.41 | 4.84 | 6.08 | -0.6 | 94.8 | 46.5 | 10.9 | 43.2 |
| 2020 | TOR | MLB | 26 | 1.38 | 4.76 | 4.71 | 0.8 | 94.4 | 47.3 | 11.1 | 44 |

## Toronto Blue Jays 2020

**Trent Thornton, continued**

### Pitch Shape vs LHH

### Pitch Shape vs RHH

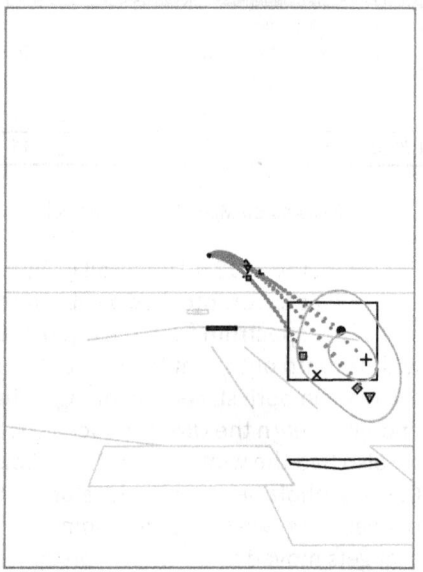

| Type | Frequency | Velocity | H Movement | V Movement |
|---|---|---|---|---|
| ● Fastball | 43.5% | 93.3 [102] | -3.1 [117] | -13.7 [106] |
| ☐ Sinker | | | | |
| + Cutter | 16.2% | 88.4 [98] | 3.9 [112] | -26.3 [92] |
| ▲ Changeup | | | | |
| ✕ Splitter | 8.9% | 83.6 [94] | -7.1 [103] | -26.8 [108] |
| ▽ Slider | 15.6% | 81 [86] | 10.6 [123] | -42.9 [72] |
| ◇ Curveball | 12.9% | 79.7 [104] | 8.2 [103] | -48 [99] |
| ⊕ Slow Curveball | | | | |
| ✱ Knuckleball | | | | |
| ▼ Screwball | | | | |

## Jacob Waguespack  RHP

Born: 11/05/93   Age: 26   Bats: R   Throws: R
Height: 6'6"   Weight: 235   Origin: Round 37, 2012 Draft (#1126 overall)

| YEAR | TEAM | LVL | AGE | W | L | SV | G | GS | IP | H | HR | BB/9 | K/9 | K | GB% | BABIP |
|------|------|-----|-----|---|---|----|----|----|-----|----|----|------|-----|----|-----|-------|
| 2017 | CLR | A+ | 23 | 6 | 5 | 1 | 24 | 10 | $68^1$ | 63 | 3 | 3.2 | 9.6 | 73 | 46% | .321 |
| 2017 | REA | AA | 23 | 3 | 2 | 0 | 7 | 6 | 37 | 37 | 2 | 3.9 | 8.5 | 35 | 50% | .327 |
| 2018 | REA | AA | 24 | 1 | 1 | 0 | 7 | 7 | $29^1$ | 31 | 0 | 4.9 | 9.5 | 31 | 59% | .352 |
| 2018 | LEH | AAA | 24 | 3 | 5 | 1 | 14 | 8 | $53^1$ | 54 | 4 | 3.4 | 8.1 | 48 | 52% | .323 |
| 2018 | BUF | AAA | 24 | 2 | 4 | 0 | 7 | 6 | $39^1$ | 47 | 3 | 2.3 | 7.6 | 33 | 54% | .346 |
| 2019 | BUF | AAA | 25 | 2 | 6 | 0 | 12 | 11 | $52^2$ | 57 | 9 | 4.3 | 8.9 | 52 | 48% | .324 |
| 2019 | TOR | MLB | 25 | 5 | 5 | 0 | 16 | 13 | 78 | 75 | 12 | 3.3 | 7.3 | 63 | 41% | .279 |
| 2020 | TOR | MLB | 26 | 3 | 3 | 0 | 38 | 3 | 53 | 55 | 10 | 3.9 | 7.4 | 44 | 44% | .289 |

Comparables: Brandon Workman, Erick Fedde, Charles Brewer

Waguespack made his MLB debut last season, the near dictionary definition of replacement level over his 78 innings, but still showed enough to get another look for the Jays rotation in 2020. If the big righty can bring his ground-ball rate back up after the bad sort of regression last season, he should be able to cement himself as a placeholder for Nate Pearson's eventual ascent. He lost more than two ticks of velocity between May and September, so it remains to be seen if the rigors of a full season agree with him. Though if he doesn't do a better job of keeping the ball in the yard, we may never truly find out.

| YEAR | TEAM | LVL | AGE | WHIP | ERA | DRA | WARP | MPH | FB% | WHF | CSP |
|------|------|-----|-----|------|-----|-----|------|-----|-----|-----|-----|
| 2017 | CLR | A+ | 23 | 1.27 | 3.29 | 4.35 | 0.6 | | | | |
| 2017 | REA | AA | 23 | 1.43 | 3.65 | 3.94 | 0.5 | | | | |
| 2018 | REA | AA | 24 | 1.60 | 3.99 | 4.90 | 0.1 | | | | |
| 2018 | LEH | AAA | 24 | 1.39 | 5.06 | 5.81 | -0.2 | | | | |
| 2018 | BUF | AAA | 24 | 1.45 | 5.03 | 5.82 | -0.2 | | | | |
| 2019 | BUF | AAA | 25 | 1.56 | 5.30 | 5.39 | 0.7 | | | | |
| 2019 | TOR | MLB | 25 | 1.33 | 4.38 | 5.66 | 0.0 | 94.6 | 48.4 | 10.8 | 46.5 |
| 2020 | TOR | MLB | 26 | 1.46 | 5.22 | 5.06 | 0.2 | 94.2 | 49.2 | 11 | 47.3 |

# Toronto Blue Jays 2020

*Jacob Waguespack, continued*

### Pitch Shape vs LHH

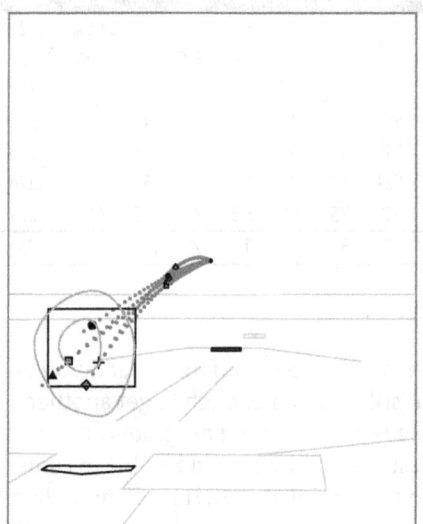

### Pitch Shape vs RHH

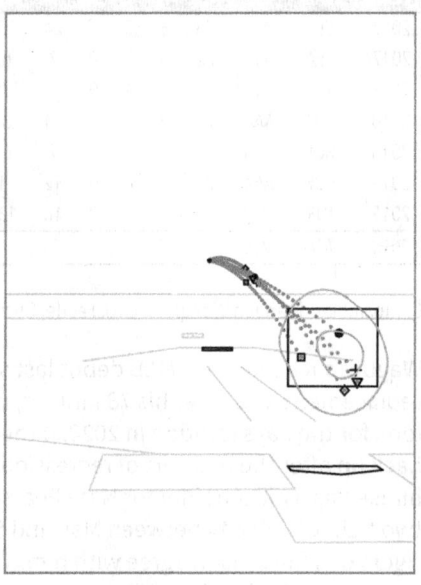

| Type | Frequency | Velocity | H Movement | V Movement |
|---|---|---|---|---|
| ● Fastball | 32.0% | 92.7 [101] | -1.4 [124] | -13.4 [107] |
| ☐ Sinker | 16.4% | 90.5 [89] | -9.3 [121] | -15.8 [116] |
| + Cutter | 24.5% | 89.4 [105] | 2.7 [105] | -22.1 [107] |
| ▲ Changeup | 8.3% | 83.3 [93] | -5.5 [127] | -23.2 [112] |
| ✕ Splitter | | | | |
| ▽ Slider | 5.2% | 85.9 [106] | 4.5 [98] | -30.4 [108] |
| ◇ Curveball | 13.7% | 78.9 [101] | 1.5 [76] | -43.6 [108] |
| ✦ Slow Curveball | | | | |
| ✳ Knuckleball | | | | |
| ▼ Screwball | | | | |

## PLAYER COMMENTS WITHOUT GRAPHS

### Griffin Conine  RF
Born: 07/11/97  Age: 22  Bats: L  Throws: R
Height: 6'1"  Weight: 200  Origin: Round 2, 2018 Draft (#52 overall)

| YEAR | TEAM | LVL | AGE | PA | R | 2B | 3B | HR | RBI | BB | K | SB | CS | AVG/OBP/SLG |
|---|---|---|---|---|---|---|---|---|---|---|---|---|---|---|
| 2018 | VAN | A- | 20 | 230 | 24 | 14 | 2 | 7 | 30 | 19 | 63 | 5 | 0 | .238/.309/.427 |
| 2019 | LNS | A | 21 | 348 | 59 | 19 | 2 | 22 | 64 | 38 | 125 | 2 | 0 | .283/.371/.576 |
| 2020 | TOR | MLB | 22 | 251 | 21 | 12 | 1 | 6 | 25 | 16 | 103 | 0 | 0 | .201/.259/.338 |

Comparables: Austin Hays, Xavier Scruggs, Kennys Vargas

The mythological griffin is half of two animals: eagle and lion. Conine's season also mashed up two starkly different halves to head-scratching results: after being suspended at the end of 2018 for a banned substance used to treat ADHD, the 22-year-old sat out the first 50 games. After returning, Conine more than delivered on his second round bona fides in Low-A. The 22 home runs were enticing, the 36 percent strikeout rate worrisome. So it goes for a hybrid.

| YEAR | TEAM | LVL | AGE | PA | DRC+ | VORP | BABIP | BRR | FRAA | WARP |
|---|---|---|---|---|---|---|---|---|---|---|
| 2018 | VAN | A- | 20 | 230 | 92 | 2.2 | .304 | -1.5 | RF(46): 10.1 | 1.1 |
| 2019 | LNS | A | 21 | 348 | 155 | 32.8 | .405 | 2.8 | RF(73): 6.2 | 3.7 |
| 2020 | TOR | MLB | 22 | 251 | 57 | -6.2 | .332 | -0.3 | RF 3 | -0.3 |

## Jordan Groshans  SS

Born: 11/10/99  Age: 20  Bats: R  Throws: R
Height: 6'3"  Weight: 205  Origin: Round 1, 2018 Draft (#12 overall)

| YEAR | TEAM | LVL | AGE | PA | R | 2B | 3B | HR | RBI | BB | K | SB | CS | AVG/OBP/SLG |
|---|---|---|---|---|---|---|---|---|---|---|---|---|---|---|
| 2018 | BLJ | RK | 18 | 159 | 17 | 12 | 0 | 4 | 39 | 13 | 29 | 0 | 0 | .331/.390/.500 |
| 2018 | BLU | RK | 18 | 48 | 4 | 1 | 0 | 1 | 4 | 2 | 8 | 0 | 0 | .182/.229/.273 |
| 2019 | LNS | A | 19 | 96 | 12 | 6 | 0 | 2 | 13 | 13 | 21 | 1 | 1 | .337/.427/.482 |
| 2020 | TOR | MLB | 20 | 251 | 23 | 12 | 0 | 5 | 25 | 19 | 70 | 1 | 0 | .238/.301/.363 |

Comparables: Trevor Story, Brendan Rodgers, Alen Hanson

Groshans has a key distinction from many of the other recent top prospects the Jays have had—rather than following in the footsteps of a first baseball generation, he is the first generation leading the next. Sort of. The year after he was taken in the first round by the Jays, his older brother, Jaxx, was a fifth-round pick of the Red Sox. Limited to just 96 plate appearances before a stress injury in his foot kept him off the field and ultimately had him shut down, the teen took control of the Midwest League by hitting for average and power along with showing a discerning eye for his age. And though his future may be more hot corner than the six, even a brief glimpse was enough to leave fans and evaluators salivating for more. Whether he starts the year with a repeat engagement in Lansing or not, the big ballparks of the Florida State League await the second-best prospect in the Toronto system in 2020.

| YEAR | TEAM | LVL | AGE | PA | DRC+ | VORP | BABIP | BRR | FRAA | WARP |
|---|---|---|---|---|---|---|---|---|---|---|
| 2018 | BLJ | RK | 18 | 159 | 147 | 14.7 | .387 | -0.8 | 3B(16): -1.2, SS(15): 0.6 | 1.1 |
| 2018 | BLU | RK | 18 | 48 | 46 | -0.6 | .194 | 0.1 | SS(6): 0.9, 3B(5): 0.0 | 0.0 |
| 2019 | LNS | A | 19 | 96 | 169 | 10.6 | .433 | -0.4 | SS(20): -1.8 | 0.9 |
| 2020 | TOR | MLB | 20 | 251 | 78 | 0.4 | .318 | -0.5 | SS 0, 3B 0 | 0.1 |

## Orelvis Martinez  SS

Born: 11/19/01  Age: 18  Bats: R  Throws: R
Height: 6'1"  Weight: 188  Origin: International Free Agent, 2018

| YEAR | TEAM | LVL | AGE | PA | R | 2B | 3B | HR | RBI | BB | K | SB | CS | AVG/OBP/SLG |
|---|---|---|---|---|---|---|---|---|---|---|---|---|---|---|
| 2019 | BLJ | RK | 17 | 163 | 20 | 8 | 5 | 7 | 32 | 14 | 29 | 2 | 0 | .275/.352/.549 |
| 2020 | TOR | MLB | 18 | 251 | 21 | 11 | 2 | 4 | 22 | 19 | 72 | 2 | 1 | .202/.272/.317 |

Comparables: Franklin Barreto, Engel Beltre, Juan Lagares

Martinez was aggressively assigned to the Gulf Coast League last season, putting him against significantly older competition in his first affiliated showing. Despite being a minor for the entire season, the left-side infielder impressed enough to make the GCL All-Star team. In the box, Martinez has enough strength to show average power right now but projects for plus once he fills out a little more. On top of that, he's a natural hitter with quick bat speed—able to both pull the ball and go the other way with authority. The Adrián Beltré comparisons have not ceased, which, weighty or not, should indicate the degree to which the teenager has impressed since inking his $3.5 million bonus. No word as of yet on whether Martinez has a problem with people touching his head.

| YEAR | TEAM | LVL | AGE | PA | DRC+ | VORP | BABIP | BRR | FRAA | WARP |
|---|---|---|---|---|---|---|---|---|---|---|
| 2019 | BLJ | RK | 17 | 163 | 140 | 18.2 | .296 | 1.1 | SS(26): -3.2, 3B(11): -2.0 | 0.8 |
| 2020 | TOR | MLB | 18 | 251 | 60 | -5.1 | .277 | 0.0 | SS -1, 3B 0 | -0.6 |

Toronto Blue Jays 2020

## Kevin Smith  SS

Born: 07/04/96   Age: 23   Bats: R   Throws: R
Height: 5'11"   Weight: 188   Origin: Round 4, 2017 Draft (#129 overall)

| YEAR | TEAM | LVL | AGE | PA | R | 2B | 3B | HR | RBI | BB | K | SB | CS | AVG/OBP/SLG |
|---|---|---|---|---|---|---|---|---|---|---|---|---|---|---|
| 2017 | BLU | RK | 20 | 283 | 43 | 25 | 1 | 8 | 43 | 16 | 70 | 9 | 0 | .271/.312/.466 |
| 2018 | LNS | A | 21 | 204 | 36 | 23 | 4 | 7 | 44 | 17 | 33 | 12 | 1 | .355/.407/.639 |
| 2018 | DUN | A+ | 21 | 371 | 57 | 8 | 2 | 18 | 49 | 23 | 88 | 17 | 5 | .274/.332/.468 |
| 2019 | NHP | AA | 22 | 468 | 49 | 22 | 2 | 19 | 61 | 29 | 151 | 11 | 6 | .209/.263/.402 |
| 2020 | TOR | MLB | 23 | 251 | 28 | 13 | 1 | 11 | 34 | 13 | 89 | 4 | 1 | .225/.271/.433 |

Comparables: Ryan O'Hearn, Lane Thomas, Zach Walters

After reaching impressive heights in two levels in 2018, Smith came back to earth and then fell below at Double-A in 2019, posting a devilish .666 OPS and following it up with a hellacious AFL stint (38 strikeouts in 68 plate appearances). Looking like less of a sure thing at short and even slowing down on the basepaths from the previous season, it was a highly disappointing year all around. With the rest of the infield prospects around him improving and solidifying themselves in major-league roles, Smith tracks to be worthy of only a cameo and not someone who brings you lasagna at work.

| YEAR | TEAM | LVL | AGE | PA | DRC+ | VORP | BABIP | BRR | FRAA | WARP |
|---|---|---|---|---|---|---|---|---|---|---|
| 2017 | BLU | RK | 20 | 283 | 95 | 18.6 | .337 | 3.9 | SS(58): 8.3 | 2.2 |
| 2018 | LNS | A | 21 | 204 | 196 | 33.7 | .397 | 3.1 | SS(24): 1.7, 3B(21): 0.7 | 3.5 |
| 2018 | DUN | A+ | 21 | 371 | 128 | 23.3 | .319 | 4.6 | SS(63): 6.9, 2B(13): 1.0 | 3.8 |
| 2019 | NHP | AA | 22 | 468 | 91 | 9.8 | .269 | 1.4 | SS(86): 0.4, 3B(18): -1.1 | 1.5 |
| 2020 | TOR | MLB | 23 | 251 | 80 | 1.8 | .307 | 0.3 | SS 3, 3B 0 | 0.5 |

## Rubén Tejada  INF

Born: 10/27/89  Age: 30  Bats: R  Throws: R
Height: 5'11"  Weight: 200  Origin: International Free Agent, 2006

| YEAR | TEAM | LVL | AGE | PA | R | 2B | 3B | HR | RBI | BB | K | SB | CS | AVG/OBP/SLG |
|---|---|---|---|---|---|---|---|---|---|---|---|---|---|---|
| 2017 | SWB | AAA | 27 | 148 | 22 | 7 | 0 | 6 | 21 | 15 | 17 | 0 | 2 | .269/.345/.462 |
| 2017 | NOR | AAA | 27 | 51 | 9 | 3 | 0 | 0 | 2 | 4 | 4 | 0 | 0 | .311/.392/.378 |
| 2017 | BAL | MLB | 27 | 124 | 17 | 6 | 0 | 0 | 5 | 8 | 15 | 0 | 0 | .230/.293/.283 |
| 2018 | NOR | AAA | 28 | 392 | 34 | 18 | 0 | 2 | 34 | 24 | 69 | 5 | 0 | .230/.291/.298 |
| 2019 | SYR | AAA | 29 | 314 | 54 | 20 | 1 | 6 | 42 | 30 | 53 | 3 | 3 | .326/.404/.471 |
| 2019 | NYN | MLB | 29 | 9 | 1 | 0 | 0 | 0 | 0 | 0 | 3 | 0 | 0 | .000/.000/.000 |
| 2020 | NYN | MLB | 30 | 251 | 23 | 11 | 0 | 4 | 24 | 21 | 51 | 1 | 0 | .233/.309/.345 |

Comparables: Terry Shumpert, Gordon Beckham, Asdrúbal Cabrera

Tejada joined Carlos Gómez as familiar faces who made their return to the team last season, after unwittingly changing baseball when he got his leg broken by Chase Utley in the 2015 NLDS. He hit quite well in Triple-A, which included a cycle, and simply making his way back to the majors was a major accomplishment for the 30-year-old. He failed to pick up a hit in his short stint back with the Mets but as always #winforruben.

| YEAR | TEAM | LVL | AGE | PA | DRC+ | VORP | BABIP | BRR | FRAA | WARP |
|---|---|---|---|---|---|---|---|---|---|---|
| 2017 | SWB | AAA | 27 | 148 | 128 | 7.4 | .266 | 0.8 | 3B(14): -0.3, SS(12): -1.1 | 1.0 |
| 2017 | NOR | AAA | 27 | 51 | 132 | 3.2 | .341 | 0.0 | SS(10): 0.5, 3B(4): -0.2 | 0.8 |
| 2017 | BAL | MLB | 27 | 124 | 87 | -3.3 | .265 | -0.1 | SS(36): -2.4, 3B(6): -0.5 | 0.1 |
| 2018 | NOR | AAA | 28 | 392 | 77 | -3.2 | .277 | 2.6 | 2B(53): -2.8, SS(27): 1.1 | 0.4 |
| 2019 | SYR | AAA | 29 | 314 | 136 | 26.0 | .385 | 0.7 | 3B(44): 0.5, SS(18): -0.8 | 2.5 |
| 2019 | NYN | MLB | 29 | 9 | 63 | -0.1 | .000 | 0.0 | SS(2): -0.1, 2B(2): -0.2 | 0.0 |
| 2020 | NYN | MLB | 30 | 251 | 76 | -0.1 | .283 | -0.5 | SS -1, 3B 0 | -0.2 |

# Toronto Blue Jays 2020

## Ryan Borucki   LHP
Born: 03/31/94   Age: 26   Bats: L   Throws: L
Height: 6'4"   Weight: 215   Origin: Round 15, 2012 Draft (#475 overall)

| YEAR | TEAM | LVL | AGE | W | L | SV | G | GS | IP | H | HR | BB/9 | K/9 | K | GB% | BABIP |
|---|---|---|---|---|---|---|---|---|---|---|---|---|---|---|---|---|
| 2017 | DUN | A+ | 23 | 6 | 5 | 0 | 19 | 18 | 98 | 95 | 5 | 2.5 | 10.0 | 109 | 52% | .342 |
| 2017 | NHP | AA | 23 | 2 | 3 | 0 | 7 | 7 | 46$^1$ | 31 | 2 | 1.6 | 8.2 | 42 | 58% | .236 |
| 2017 | BUF | AAA | 23 | 0 | 0 | 0 | 1 | 1 | 6 | 6 | 0 | 1.5 | 9.0 | 6 | 50% | .375 |
| 2018 | BUF | AAA | 24 | 6 | 5 | 0 | 13 | 13 | 77 | 62 | 6 | 3.3 | 6.8 | 58 | 52% | .255 |
| 2018 | TOR | MLB | 24 | 4 | 6 | 0 | 17 | 17 | 97$^2$ | 96 | 7 | 3.0 | 6.2 | 67 | 49% | .291 |
| 2019 | BUF | AAA | 25 | 1 | 0 | 0 | 2 | 2 | 11 | 11 | 4 | 2.5 | 7.4 | 9 | 42% | .241 |
| 2019 | TOR | MLB | 25 | 0 | 1 | 0 | 2 | 2 | 6$^2$ | 15 | 2 | 8.1 | 8.1 | 6 | 39% | .500 |
| 2020 | TOR | MLB | 26 | 4 | 5 | 0 | 15 | 15 | 73 | 89 | 12 | 3.7 | 6.5 | 52 | 46% | .326 |

Comparables: Steven Brault, Anthony Banda, Matt Hall

The story, once again with Borucki, was injuries. The 25-year-old has been racking up a health record that would make Mark Prior take note, and tossed fewer than 25 innings across four different levels last season. After elbow inflammation kept him out of roughly the season's first half, Borucki built up (and worked through various rehab stints) for two starts in the back half of July before his elbow again started acting up. One surgery for bone spurs later and the sophomore's season ended, a huge letdown after an encouraging debut and another contributing factor in the oft-pitiable Jays rotation. The lefty's elbow is purported to have a clean bill of health entering the new year, so here's to the rest of him staying healthy as well.

| YEAR | TEAM | LVL | AGE | WHIP | ERA | DRA | WARP | MPH | FB% | WHF | CSP |
|---|---|---|---|---|---|---|---|---|---|---|---|
| 2017 | DUN | A+ | 23 | 1.24 | 3.58 | 4.81 | 0.5 | | | | |
| 2017 | NHP | AA | 23 | 0.84 | 1.94 | 2.20 | 1.6 | | | | |
| 2017 | BUF | AAA | 23 | 1.17 | 0.00 | 3.93 | 0.1 | | | | |
| 2018 | BUF | AAA | 24 | 1.17 | 3.27 | 3.57 | 1.7 | | | | |
| 2018 | TOR | MLB | 24 | 1.32 | 3.87 | 4.53 | 0.9 | 93.4 | 58.7 | 8.7 | 49.1 |
| 2019 | BUF | AAA | 25 | 1.27 | 4.91 | 5.11 | 0.2 | | | | |
| 2019 | TOR | MLB | 25 | 3.15 | 10.80 | 8.81 | -0.2 | 94.2 | 52.3 | 9 | 44.1 |
| 2020 | TOR | MLB | 26 | 1.63 | 6.34 | 5.94 | -0.3 | 93.1 | 59 | 8.9 | 47.2 |

## Adam Kloffenstein   RHP

Born: 08/25/00   Age: 19   Bats: R   Throws: R  
Height: 6'5"   Weight: 243   Origin: Round 3, 2018 Draft (#88 overall)

| YEAR | TEAM | LVL | AGE | W | L | SV | G | GS | IP | H | HR | BB/9 | K/9 | K | GB% | BABIP |
|---|---|---|---|---|---|---|---|---|---|---|---|---|---|---|---|---|
| 2019 | VAN | A- | 18 | 4 | 4 | 0 | 13 | 13 | 64$^1$ | 47 | 4 | 3.2 | 9.0 | 64 | 61% | .262 |
| 2020 | TOR | MLB | 19 | 2 | 2 | 0 | 33 | 0 | 35 | 35 | 6 | 4.4 | 7.7 | 30 | 52% | .288 |

Comparables: Jenrry Mejia, Arodys Vizcaíno, Jamie Callahan

Shortly after he was drafted two summers ago, Kloffenstein presented former burly right-handed pitching prospect Nate Pearson with an unusual proposal: "Hey man, I'm just gonna follow you around a little bit for the next couple days. Don't take it weird. I'm not gonna be wearing your shoes." Weird the phrasing might have been, but the then-17-year-old's willingness to put himself out there in the interest of furthering himself—in this case, via familiarizing himself with the rituals and routines of his new organization's most highly-regarded pitching prospect—portends well for the teenager's development. Kloffenstein impressed in short-season ball, albeit with slightly less punch to his heater than he showed as an amateur, giving reason to believe he can stick as a starter and potentially follow—metaphorically or not—the path Pearson's performance has blazed.

| YEAR | TEAM | LVL | AGE | WHIP | ERA | DRA | WARP | MPH | FB% | WHF | CSP |
|---|---|---|---|---|---|---|---|---|---|---|---|
| 2019 | VAN | A- | 18 | 1.09 | 2.24 | 3.03 | 1.6 | | | | |
| 2020 | TOR | MLB | 19 | 1.48 | 5.08 | 5.02 | 0.1 | | | | |

Toronto Blue Jays 2020

### Alek Manoah  RHP
Born: 01/09/98   Age: 22   Bats: R   Throws: R
Height: 6'6"   Weight: 260   Origin: Round 1, 2019 Draft (#11 overall)

| YEAR | TEAM | LVL | AGE | W | L | SV | G | GS | IP | H | HR | BB/9 | K/9 | K | GB% | BABIP |
|---|---|---|---|---|---|---|---|---|---|---|---|---|---|---|---|---|
| 2019 | VAN | A- | 21 | 0 | 1 | 0 | 6 | 6 | 17 | 13 | 1 | 2.6 | 14.3 | 27 | 30% | .379 |
| 2020 | TOR | MLB | 22 | 2 | 2 | 0 | 33 | 0 | 35 | 36 | 6 | 3.7 | 9.9 | 39 | 36% | .320 |

Comparables: Radhames Liz, Michael Stutes, Jeremy Hefner

One of the most talented arms in the 2019 draft class, the 11th-overall pick has an impressive fastball-slider combo that bodes well for his chances of reaching and sticking at the highest level. Manoah is solidly built and throws hard, but is going to need to develop a pitch to keep lefties from tagging him as he climbs through the minors. Even if his abbreviated pro debut, he allowed an OPS more than 250 points higher when facing opposite-handed hitters. Having turned 22 at the start of the year, Manoah may also have the benefit of a bit more development time than most college arms are allotted—time he could use to find the feel for a change. It's also good to have long-term goals, as last May he told the Miami Herald he plans "to play 10 years in the big leagues, and then hop in the broadcast booth with Alex Rodriguez."

| YEAR | TEAM | LVL | AGE | WHIP | ERA | DRA | WARP | MPH | FB% | WHF | CSP |
|---|---|---|---|---|---|---|---|---|---|---|---|
| 2019 | VAN | A- | 21 | 1.06 | 2.65 | 3.15 | 0.4 | | | | |
| 2020 | TOR | MLB | 22 | 1.43 | 4.96 | 4.93 | 0.1 | | | | |

## Eric Pardinho  RHP

Born: 01/05/01  Age: 19  Bats: R  Throws: R
Height: 5'10"  Weight: 155  Origin: International Free Agent, 2017

| YEAR | TEAM | LVL | AGE | W | L | SV | G | GS | IP | H | HR | BB/9 | K/9 | K | GB% | BABIP |
|------|------|-----|-----|---|---|----|----|----|------|----|----|------|------|----|-----|-------|
| 2018 | BLU | RK | 17 | 4 | 3 | 0 | 11 | 11 | 50 | 37 | 5 | 2.9 | 11.5 | 64 | 47% | .274 |
| 2019 | LNS | A | 18 | 1 | 1 | 0 | 7 | 7 | 33² | 29 | 1 | 3.5 | 8.0 | 30 | 44% | .304 |
| 2020 | TOR | MLB | 19 | 2 | 2 | 0 | 33 | 0 | 35 | 35 | 6 | 4.0 | 7.9 | 31 | 41% | .293 |

Comparables: Jordan Lyles, Pedro Avila, Lewis Thorpe

The bad: Pardinho pitched fewer total innings in 2019 than the prior year after elbow soreness shut him down in spring training. The Jays took an extraordinarily cautious approach in handling the Brazilian sensation, keeping him out of action until June and then ending his season six weeks later. The good: the diminutive righty will not turn 20 until after the 2020 season, and he impressed in Low-A ball even with a compacted schedule. He'll need to add to his frame and show some extra durability to remain a starter, but there has been precious little to indicate Pardinho cannot deliver on the incredible promise he showed as a 15-year-old pitching in the World Baseball Classic.

| YEAR | TEAM | LVL | AGE | WHIP | ERA | DRA | WARP | MPH | FB% | WHF | CSP |
|------|------|-----|-----|------|------|------|------|-----|-----|-----|-----|
| 2018 | BLU | RK | 17 | 1.06 | 2.88 | 1.45 | 2.5 | | | | |
| 2019 | LNS | A | 18 | 1.25 | 2.41 | 4.68 | 0.2 | | | | |
| 2020 | TOR | MLB | 19 | 1.45 | 4.92 | 4.92 | 0.1 | | | | |

Toronto Blue Jays 2020

## Nate Pearson  RHP

Born: 08/20/96   Age: 23   Bats: R   Throws: R
Height: 6'6"   Weight: 245   Origin: Round 1, 2017 Draft (#28 overall)

| YEAR | TEAM | LVL | AGE | W | L | SV | G | GS | IP | H | HR | BB/9 | K/9 | K | GB% | BABIP |
|---|---|---|---|---|---|---|---|---|---|---|---|---|---|---|---|---|
| 2017 | VAN | A- | 20 | 0 | 0 | 0 | 7 | 7 | 19 | 6 | 0 | 2.4 | 11.4 | 24 | 40% | .158 |
| 2019 | DUN | A+ | 22 | 3 | 0 | 0 | 6 | 6 | 21 | 10 | 2 | 1.3 | 15.0 | 35 | 35% | .229 |
| 2019 | NHP | AA | 22 | 1 | 4 | 0 | 16 | 16 | 62$^2$ | 41 | 4 | 3.0 | 9.9 | 69 | 40% | .250 |
| 2019 | BUF | AAA | 22 | 1 | 0 | 0 | 3 | 3 | 18 | 12 | 2 | 1.5 | 7.5 | 15 | 44% | .208 |
| 2020 | TOR | MLB | 23 | 3 | 3 | 0 | 14 | 8 | 47 | 46 | 8 | 3.6 | 10.0 | 52 | 40% | .313 |

Comparables: Clay Buchholz, Marco Gonzales, Daniel Hudson

Limited to just a single outing in the 2018 regular season, the impetus was on Pearson to perform last year, particularly with the system's best two prospects graduating and the organization having an obvious dearth of premiere or even reliable pitching. Pearson is not just a starter but an education company, though, and he did plenty of both learning and schooling in 2019. Hilariously overqualified for High-A, he steamrolled through Double-A as well, even acquitting himself well in three starts at Buffalo to finish the season. In the end, the year was a near-unqualified success; surpassing 100 innings put to rest any lingering concerns from the freak injury that cost Pearson 2018, and he appears on the cusp of breaking into the majors later this year—he gave evaluators little choice but to vaunt him to the top of org lists with his dominating season.

| YEAR | TEAM | LVL | AGE | WHIP | ERA | DRA | WARP | MPH | FB% | WHF | CSP |
|---|---|---|---|---|---|---|---|---|---|---|---|
| 2017 | VAN | A- | 20 | 0.58 | 0.95 | 1.01 | 0.9 | | | | |
| 2019 | DUN | A+ | 22 | 0.62 | 0.86 | 1.59 | 0.9 | | | | |
| 2019 | NHP | AA | 22 | 0.99 | 2.59 | 3.16 | 1.4 | | | | |
| 2019 | BUF | AAA | 22 | 0.83 | 3.00 | 3.61 | 0.5 | | | | |
| 2020 | TOR | MLB | 23 | 1.40 | 4.72 | 4.70 | 0.4 | | | | |

## Simeon Woods Richardson   RHP

Born: 09/27/00   Age: 19   Bats: R   Throws: R
Height: 6'3"   Weight: 210   Origin: Round 2, 2018 Draft (#48 overall)

| YEAR | TEAM | LVL | AGE | W | L | SV | G | GS | IP | H | HR | BB/9 | K/9 | K | GB% | BABIP |
|---|---|---|---|---|---|---|---|---|---|---|---|---|---|---|---|---|
| 2018 | MTS | RK | 17 | 1 | 0 | 1 | 5 | 2 | 11$^1$ | 9 | 0 | 3.2 | 11.9 | 15 | 50% | .321 |
| 2018 | KNG | RK | 17 | 0 | 0 | 0 | 2 | 2 | 6 | 6 | 1 | 0.0 | 16.5 | 11 | 38% | .417 |
| 2019 | COL | A | 18 | 3 | 8 | 0 | 20 | 20 | 78$^1$ | 78 | 5 | 2.0 | 11.1 | 97 | 50% | .356 |
| 2019 | DUN | A+ | 18 | 3 | 2 | 0 | 6 | 6 | 28$^1$ | 18 | 1 | 2.2 | 9.2 | 29 | 38% | .254 |
| 2020 | TOR | MLB | 19 | 2 | 2 | 0 | 33 | 0 | 35 | 35 | 5 | 4.1 | 9.2 | 36 | 44% | .306 |

Comparables: Jordan Lyles, Lewis Thorpe, Mike Soroka

In an interview before he was drafted in 2018, Woods Richardson said "I like being in control and making batters uncomfortable." Presumably, the 19-year-old and one-half of Toronto's return for Marcus Stroman is enjoying his new responsibility; taking control of the trade and making Brodie Van Wagenen uncomfortable. Anthony Kay may have the higher floor, but it's Woods Richardson with the vastly superior ceiling. After sputtering through a tough May, the Texan dominated both the South Atlantic and Florida State Leagues at the ripe age of 18, holding opposing batters to a .197/.246/.283 batting line over his last 70-plus innings of the season. Armed with a fastball that sits in the mid-90s but hit triple-digits from time to time and a curveball that gave hitters 4-5 years older than him fits, Woods Richardson has one of the most exciting one-two punches in the lower minors. The lack of a third pitch brings bullpen creep with it, but given he'll still be a teenager for the entirety of 2020, that concern can wait.

| YEAR | TEAM | LVL | AGE | WHIP | ERA | DRA | WARP | MPH | FB% | WHF | CSP |
|---|---|---|---|---|---|---|---|---|---|---|---|
| 2018 | MTS | RK | 17 | 1.15 | 0.00 | 1.39 | 0.6 | | | | |
| 2018 | KNG | RK | 17 | 1.00 | 4.50 | 1.97 | 0.3 | | | | |
| 2019 | COL | A | 18 | 1.21 | 4.25 | 5.04 | 0.1 | | | | |
| 2019 | DUN | A+ | 18 | 0.88 | 2.54 | 3.05 | 0.7 | | | | |
| 2020 | TOR | MLB | 19 | 1.44 | 4.78 | 4.83 | 0.1 | | | | |

# Toronto Blue Jays 2020

## Shun Yamaguchi   RHP
Born: 07/11/87   Age: 32   Bats: R   Throws: R
Height: 6'2"   Weight: 198   Origin: International Free Agent, 2019

The 2019 Blue Jays burned through rotation options more frequently than Emily Gilmore changed housemaids. Predictably, they spent the offseason tweaking their starting five. Yamaguchi might be the most unknown of the additions. His track record in Japan saw him serve as a frontline starter for much of the last seven years. He doesn't have great stuff—his fastball averages 90 mph and neither of his breaking balls are what you would classify as high-grade offerings—but his splitter is a legitimate weapon and he should serve as a useful reliever if nothing else.

# LINEOUTS

## Hitters

| HITTER | POS | TEAM | LVL | AGE | PA | R | 2B | 3B | HR | RBI | BB | K | SB | CS | AVG/OBP/SLG | DRC+ | WARP |
|---|---|---|---|---|---|---|---|---|---|---|---|---|---|---|---|---|---|
| Anthony Alford | CF | TOR | MLB | 24 | 30 | 3 | 0 | 0 | 1 | 1 | 1 | 11 | 2 | 0 | .179/.233/.286 | 66 | 0.0 |
|  | CF | BUF | AAA | 24 | 319 | 46 | 16 | 3 | 7 | 37 | 31 | 94 | 22 | 8 | .259/.343/.411 | 95 | 0.8 |
| Jonathan Davis | CF | TOR | MLB | 27 | 95 | 8 | 1 | 0 | 2 | 6 | 5 | 24 | 3 | 1 | .181/.266/.265 | 75 | -0.2 |
|  | CF | BUF | AAA | 27 | 352 | 64 | 19 | 3 | 10 | 36 | 40 | 83 | 13 | 4 | .262/.382/.449 | 122 | 2.1 |
| Santiago Espinal | MI | BUF | AAA | 24 | 112 | 11 | 6 | 0 | 2 | 14 | 7 | 23 | 2 | 2 | .317/.360/.433 | 101 | 0.6 |
|  | MI | NHP | AA | 24 | 409 | 46 | 21 | 1 | 5 | 57 | 35 | 50 | 10 | 11 | .278/.343/.381 | 126 | 3.0 |
| Alen Hanson | 2B | BUF | AAA | 26 | 180 | 19 | 3 | 1 | 3 | 18 | 9 | 39 | 7 | 2 | .187/.232/.271 | 31 | -0.9 |
|  | 2B | TOR | MLB | 26 | 48 | 5 | 0 | 0 | 0 | 4 | 3 | 17 | 1 | 0 | .163/.229/.163 | 59 | -0.2 |
| Miguel Hiraldo | 3B | BLU | Rk+ | 18 | 256 | 43 | 20 | 1 | 7 | 37 | 14 | 36 | 11 | 3 | .300/.348/.481 | 125 | 1.7 |
| Leonardo Jimenez | SS | BLU | Rk+ | 18 | 245 | 34 | 13 | 2 | 0 | 22 | 21 | 42 | 2 | 1 | .298/.377/.377 | 120 | 1.6 |
| Alejandro Kirk | C | DUN | A+ | 20 | 276 | 26 | 25 | 0 | 4 | 36 | 38 | 31 | 2 | 0 | .288/.395/.446 | 154 | 2.4 |
|  | C | LNS | A | 20 | 96 | 15 | 6 | 1 | 3 | 8 | 18 | 8 | 1 | 0 | .299/.427/.519 | 162 | 1.1 |
| Gabriel Moreno | C | LNS | A | 19 | 341 | 47 | 17 | 5 | 12 | 52 | 22 | 38 | 7 | 1 | .280/.337/.485 | 130 | 2.5 |
| Samad Taylor | 2B | DUN | A+ | 20 | 384 | 48 | 20 | 3 | 7 | 38 | 49 | 107 | 26 | 10 | .216/.325/.364 | 98 | 1.1 |
| Breyvic Valera | INF | SWB | AAA | 27 | 348 | 44 | 18 | 2 | 13 | 49 | 34 | 34 | 8 | 6 | .315/.388/.515 | 130 | 2.1 |
|  | INF | NYA | MLB | 27 | 37 | 5 | 1 | 1 | 0 | 3 | 4 | 5 | 0 | 0 | .219/.324/.313 | 91 | 0.2 |
|  | INF | TOR | MLB | 27 | 15 | 2 | 1 | 0 | 1 | 3 | 0 | 2 | 0 | 0 | .267/.267/.533 | 102 | 0.0 |
|  | INF | SAC | AAA | 27 | 92 | 10 | 3 | 0 | 1 | 7 | 16 | 10 | 2 | 1 | .257/.396/.338 | 104 | 0.5 |
| Forrest Wall | CF | BUF | AAA | 23 | 53 | 9 | 3 | 0 | 2 | 4 | 6 | 14 | 1 | 0 | .255/.340/.447 | 99 | 0.2 |
|  | CF | NHP | AA | 23 | 469 | 70 | 27 | 4 | 9 | 41 | 49 | 109 | 13 | 8 | .270/.353/.419 | 134 | 3.8 |
| Chavez Young | OF | DUN | A+ | 21 | 448 | 53 | 17 | 4 | 6 | 43 | 35 | 102 | 24 | 11 | .247/.315/.354 | 85 | 0.9 |

"Injury-prone" is a label too hastily affixed, but applies to **Anthony Alford**, who has never reached 500 plate appearances in a season and looks overmatched in the majors.  ⓘ **Jonathan Davis** made one of the catches of the year in his native

center, ranging deep and to the left before making a full-extension Superman catch. Unfortunately the rest of the season was much more Clark Kent, with the slight right-handed outfielder failing to break .300 in any triple slash category.
ⓧ **Santiago Espinal** made history in June as the first player in affiliated ball this century to steal home for a walk-off victory. He also impressed so much at Double-A that he was named an Eastern League All-Star and earned a promotion to Buffalo in August. ⓧ All anyone could talk about when discussing Triple-A in 2019 was offense, which must have been frustrating to **Alen Hanson** as he barely broke a .500 OPS in 180 plate appearances with Buffalo. ⓧ **Miguel Hiraldo** is not mimicking the meteoric path a few fellow Blue Jays prospects (and international signees) have, but there's still a lot to be encouraged by. The bat impressed in the Appalachian League, though a future at shortstop is looking less probable than at second base. ⓧ This teenage glove appears to have turned around enough to box out teammate Miguel Hiraldo at the six more often than not, qualifying as a mutation. At the plate, though, while he has the eye of a ninja, **Leonardo Jimenez** doesn't quite have that turtle power yet, as he still stands without a professional homer. ⓧ With a build more Kirk Gibson than romance novel, **Alejandro Kirk** will need to continue hitting and catching to prove his short and stout frame can succeed at the upper levels of affiliated ball. ⓧ Catchers who can hit are like Starburst: a juicy contradiction. **Gabriel Moreno** still has a ways to go before he'll have a chance to swat in the majors, but his 11 percent strikeout rate as a teen in the Midwest League was another indication this is an advanced bat in the making. ⓧ The second piece (after Thomas Pannone) Toronto acquired in the Joe Smith trade, the Blue Jays have moved **Samad Taylor** aggressively and the second baseman has rewarded their actions by holding his own despite his relative youth. ⓧ **Breyvic Valera** is destined to jump from team to team, filling in defensively whenever the injury bug strikes or a team is tanking as a switch-hitter who works his walks. ⓧ It's been a long road for **Forrest Wall**, the former Rockies first-round pick in 2014, but he finally reached Triple-A at the end of the 2019 season and the strides he's made with his center field defense give him a fighting chance at a fourth outfielder role. ⓧ Bearing the surnames of two former AL West All-Star infielders, **Chavez Young** plays against type in the outfield but he plays it well. However, the 39th-round pick struggled at the plate while attempting to navigate the better arms throughout the Florida State League.

# Toronto Blue Jays 2020

## Pitchers

| PITCHER | TEAM | LVL | AGE | W | L | SV | G | GS | IP | H | HR | BB/9 | K/9 | K | GB% | WHIP | ERA | DRA | WARP |
|---|---|---|---|---|---|---|---|---|---|---|---|---|---|---|---|---|---|---|---|
| Travis Bergen | SAC | AAA | 25 | 0 | 0 | 1 | 15 | 0 | 16$^2$ | 13 | 2 | 5.4 | 8.1 | 15 | 46% | 1.38 | 3.78 | 4.24 | 0.3 |
| | SFN | MLB | 25 | 2 | 0 | 0 | 21 | 0 | 19$^2$ | 18 | 4 | 4.1 | 8.2 | 18 | 39% | 1.37 | 5.49 | 5.27 | 0.0 |
| Maximo Castillo | DUN | A+ | 20 | 11 | 5 | 0 | 24 | 24 | 130$^1$ | 115 | 8 | 1.9 | 7.9 | 114 | 39% | 1.10 | 2.69 | 3.81 | 1.9 |
| A.J. Cole | COH | AAA | 27 | 0 | 1 | 2 | 13 | 0 | 17 | 10 | 2 | 2.6 | 11.1 | 21 | 36% | 0.88 | 3.18 | 2.73 | 0.6 |
| | CLE | MLB | 27 | 3 | 1 | 1 | 25 | 0 | 26 | 31 | 4 | 2.8 | 10.4 | 30 | 31% | 1.50 | 3.81 | 6.45 | -0.3 |
| Yennsy Diaz | NHP | AA | 22 | 11 | 9 | 0 | 26 | 24 | 144$^1$ | 125 | 12 | 3.3 | 7.2 | 116 | 42% | 1.23 | 3.74 | 4.82 | 0.2 |
| | TOR | MLB | 22 | 0 | 0 | 0 | 1 | 0 | 0$^2$ | 1 | 0 | 54.0 | 0.0 | 0 | 33% | 7.50 | 27.00 | 10.53 | 0.0 |
| Ryan Dull | SWB | AAA | 29 | 1 | 0 | 0 | 4 | 0 | 6$^2$ | 3 | 1 | 1.4 | 5.4 | 4 | 22% | 0.60 | 2.70 | 3.19 | 0.2 |
| | LVG | AAA | 29 | 1 | 4 | 4 | 30 | 0 | 39$^2$ | 43 | 6 | 2.9 | 11.3 | 50 | 37% | 1.41 | 5.45 | 3.73 | 1.0 |
| | TOR | MLB | 29 | 0 | 0 | 0 | 1 | 0 | 1$^1$ | 1 | 1 | 0.0 | 20.2 | 3 | 0% | 0.75 | 6.75 | 3.35 | 0.0 |
| | NYA | MLB | 29 | 0 | 0 | 0 | 3 | 0 | 2$^1$ | 5 | 0 | 11.6 | 15.4 | 4 | 25% | 3.43 | 19.29 | 9.64 | -0.1 |
| | OAK | MLB | 29 | 0 | 0 | 0 | 7 | 0 | 9 | 19 | 4 | 4.0 | 8.0 | 8 | 32% | 2.56 | 12.00 | 8.59 | -0.3 |
| Ryan Feierabend | BUF | AAA | 33 | 6 | 5 | 0 | 14 | 12 | 68$^1$ | 77 | 19 | 2.8 | 7.0 | 53 | 38% | 1.43 | 5.53 | 5.79 | 0.6 |
| | TOR | MLB | 33 | 0 | 1 | 0 | 2 | 1 | 5$^2$ | 11 | 2 | 1.6 | 6.4 | 4 | 42% | 2.12 | 11.12 | 6.35 | 0.0 |
| Thomas Hatch | TEN | AA | 24 | 4 | 10 | 0 | 21 | 21 | 100 | 104 | 13 | 3.3 | 8.4 | 93 | 38% | 1.41 | 4.59 | 5.63 | -0.8 |
| | NHP | AA | 24 | 2 | 3 | 0 | 6 | 6 | 35$^1$ | 25 | 5 | 0.5 | 8.7 | 34 | 52% | 0.76 | 2.80 | 3.71 | 0.5 |
| Kyle Johnston | POT | A+ | 22 | 9 | 9 | 0 | 20 | 20 | 105 | 92 | 7 | 3.2 | 8.6 | 100 | 44% | 1.23 | 4.03 | 4.93 | 0.1 |
| | DUN | A+ | 22 | 1 | 3 | 0 | 6 | 4 | 19$^2$ | 18 | 2 | 9.2 | 5.9 | 13 | 46% | 1.93 | 10.07 | 8.53 | -0.8 |
| Nick Kingham | TOR | MLB | 27 | 3 | 1 | 0 | 11 | 0 | 21 | 24 | 4 | 3.4 | 6.0 | 14 | 48% | 1.52 | 3.00 | 4.92 | 0.1 |
| | PIT | MLB | 27 | 1 | 1 | 1 | 14 | 4 | 34$^2$ | 54 | 7 | 4.4 | 8.3 | 32 | 40% | 2.05 | 9.87 | 8.39 | -1.1 |
| Jackson McClelland | NHP | AA | 24 | 0 | 2 | 1 | 32 | 0 | 42$^1$ | 33 | 4 | 4.5 | 8.9 | 42 | 32% | 1.28 | 2.98 | 4.87 | -0.1 |
| | BUF | AAA | 24 | 0 | 0 | 0 | 11 | 0 | 15 | 12 | 2 | 6.6 | 8.4 | 14 | 28% | 1.53 | 6.00 | 4.41 | 0.3 |
| Justin Miller | FRE | AAA | 32 | 0 | 0 | 0 | 9 | 0 | 12$^2$ | 9 | 3 | 2.1 | 11.4 | 16 | 23% | 0.95 | 2.84 | 3.25 | 0.4 |
| | WAS | MLB | 32 | 1 | 0 | 0 | 17 | 0 | 15$^2$ | 16 | 5 | 2.3 | 6.3 | 11 | 23% | 1.28 | 4.02 | 7.34 | -0.3 |
| Patrick Murphy | NHP | AA | 24 | 4 | 7 | 0 | 18 | 18 | 84 | 75 | 7 | 2.9 | 9.2 | 86 | 53% | 1.21 | 4.71 | 4.44 | 0.5 |
| Hector Perez | NHP | AA | 23 | 7 | 6 | 0 | 26 | 24 | 121$^1$ | 130 | 9 | 5.0 | 8.7 | 117 | 40% | 1.62 | 4.60 | 6.70 | -2.6 |
| Jackson Rees | LNS | A | 24 | 2 | 0 | 2 | 14 | 0 | 25$^1$ | 13 | 0 | 1.4 | 15.6 | 44 | 68% | 0.67 | 0.36 | 1.79 | 0.9 |
| | DUN | A+ | 24 | 3 | 2 | 7 | 25 | 0 | 36$^1$ | 27 | 1 | 2.7 | 10.9 | 44 | 61% | 1.05 | 0.99 | 3.53 | 0.5 |
| Clayton Richard | TOR | MLB | 35 | 1 | 5 | 0 | 10 | 10 | 45$^1$ | 53 | 9 | 3.6 | 4.4 | 22 | 55% | 1.57 | 5.96 | 7.11 | -0.7 |
| Brock Stewart | BUF | AAA | 27 | 1 | 1 | 0 | 2 | 1 | 8$^1$ | 13 | 3 | 3.2 | 6.5 | 6 | 48% | 1.92 | 7.56 | 6.90 | 0.0 |
| | OKL | AAA | 27 | 5 | 7 | 0 | 17 | 16 | 76 | 97 | 19 | 4.7 | 7.9 | 67 | 41% | 1.80 | 7.34 | 7.22 | -0.4 |
| | TOR | MLB | 27 | 4 | 0 | 0 | 10 | 0 | 21$^2$ | 28 | 9 | 2.5 | 6.6 | 16 | 35% | 1.57 | 8.31 | 9.65 | -1.0 |
| | LAN | MLB | 27 | 0 | 0 | 0 | 3 | 0 | 4 | 9 | 2 | 4.5 | 6.8 | 3 | 44% | 2.75 | 18.00 | 4.57 | 0.0 |

| PITCHER | TEAM | LVL | AGE | W | L | SV | G | GS | IP | H | HR | BB/9 | K/9 | K | GB% | WHIP | ERA | DRA | WARP |
|---|---|---|---|---|---|---|---|---|---|---|---|---|---|---|---|---|---|---|---|
| Kendall Williams | BLJ | Rk | 18 | 0 | 0 | 0 | 6 | 5 | 16 | 6 | 0 | 3.9 | 10.7 | 19 | 36% | 0.81 | 1.12 | 1.93 | 0.7 |
| Josh Winckowski | LNS | A | 21 | 6 | 3 | 0 | 13 | 13 | $73^2$ | 62 | 3 | 3.2 | 8.7 | 71 | 56% | 1.19 | 2.32 | 3.74 | 1.3 |
|  | DUN | A+ | 21 | 4 | 5 | 1 | 11 | 10 | $53^2$ | 48 | 5 | 2.9 | 6.2 | 37 | 50% | 1.21 | 3.19 | 3.98 | 0.7 |
| T.J. Zeuch | DUN | A+ | 23 | 0 | 0 | 0 | 2 | 2 | $8^2$ | 7 | 0 | 2.1 | 12.5 | 12 | 43% | 1.04 | 4.15 | 2.19 | 0.3 |
|  | BUF | AAA | 23 | 4 | 3 | 0 | 13 | 13 | 78 | 70 | 6 | 3.7 | 4.5 | 39 | 58% | 1.31 | 3.69 | 3.95 | 2.1 |
|  | TOR | MLB | 23 | 1 | 2 | 0 | 5 | 3 | $22^2$ | 22 | 2 | 4.4 | 7.9 | 20 | 48% | 1.46 | 4.76 | 5.30 | 0.1 |

A Rule 5 pick who spent most of his year in the Giants organization, **Travis Bergen** was returned to the Blue Jays. The 26-year-old southpaw has low-90s heat and leans on a curveball as his secondary offering. ⓧ **Maximo Castillo** came in third among Florida State League starters in both innings pitched and ERA and has progressed purposefully since his 2015 signing. ⓧ **A.J. Cole** didn't go platinum with no features, but he did utilize a new slider-heavy approach to strike out a quarter of the batters he faced before a shoulder impingement shortened his season. ⓧ **Yennsy Díaz** made his MLB debut on August 4th and recorded two outs of the seven batters he faced, but his four walks gave him 54.0 walks per nine in his abbreviated rookie season. He also topped out near 98, tossed a full season of average innings in Double A and is still just 23 years old, so he'll have opportunities to bring that egregious number down. ⓧ Americans have been been desensitized to violence by a variety of parameters but that doesn't mean we should feel good about shipping **Ryan Dull** to Canada just to see how they react to what batters do to his pitches. ⓧ It had been five years since **Ryan Feierabend** last appeared in the majors when the Jays added him to their roster last May. The knuckleballer was on the roster six days, but at least it got him his first comment in a decade! ⓧ A former rising prospect in the Cubs system with a big fastball, **Thomas Hatch** was sent up North when the Jays traded David Phelps to Chicago. No word on if the transition from Double-A Tennessee to his new affiliate in New Hampshire made Hatch chilly. ⓧ Toronto's return for Daniel Hudson, the Nationals' sixth-round pick from 2017, and perhaps the most tenuous of GM Ross Atkins' superior "42 years of team control" presumption, **Kyle Johnston** has yet to master High-A (4.97 ERA) in three separate stints dating back to 2018. ⓧ **Nick Kingham** finally met his fate in the bullpen last year, but the transition didn't take, and the 28-year-old was thrice designated. It appears the high end of his outcome range was taken by his 2015 Tommy John surgery, but the SK Wyverns have made a small bet that his fastball will look better in Korea. ⓧ **Jackson McClelland** could not maintain the sky-high punchout rates that earned him a promotion to Double-A at the end of 2018, but he still showed enough to be promoted to Triple-A for the end of 2019. If this pattern holds, expect to see the 25-year-old struggle to strike out six per nine and still be called up by year's end. ⓧ At 28, **Julian Merryweather** is not slightly older than the rest of the Blue Jays pitching prospects, but that's in part due to his elbow being a fairweather friend with Tommy John surgery costing him nearly all of the last two seasons. ⓧ Unmemorable is actually the highest compliment one can give a member of the Nationals bullpen in the first half. **Justin Miller** sure was there, featuring an unspectacular fastball-slider arsenal and posting boring numbers across the board before being sent into hibernation with the Fresno Grizzlies for the remainder of the season. ⚾ How unusual can a toe tap be? Extremely, in **Patrick Murphy**'s case—he's a pitcher. This quirk became a major problem in early June when Murphy was informed that his timing mechanism was illegal, representing a second step towards home. Those two steps forward became one step back: his ERA doubled amidst an emergency delivery overhaul. ⚾ As long as **Hector Perez** keeps putting up walk rates at or above five per nine innings, Annuals will keep forecasting a move to the bullpen. If the Blue Jays don't pull the plug soon, their paucity of starters might force Perez and his lack of control into an uncomfortable and possibly unwatchable situation. ⚾ In 2018, **Jackson Rees** was undrafted out of the University of Hawaii, signing with the Blue Jays a week after the draft for a lowly $1,000. A year later, he was one of the most dominant relievers in the low minors and a Fall Star in the AFL on the strength of his deception and a funky slider that hitters have trouble tracking. ⚾ Last September 12th, the Blue Jays official Twitter wished **Clayton Richard** a happy 36th birthday with the help of sponsor (and still-extant-in-Canada) Toys R Us, differentiable from the defunct US incarnation thanks to a handy maple leaf in the R's counter. That same day, the team released Richard, proving that classic Canadian hospitality does not translate to American-helmed front offices. ⚾ **Brock Stewart**'s 2019 featured two blue teams spread across a border, and he underwhelmed for both; the multi-inning role Toronto tried the onetime Dodgers product in took no better than his sporadic usage across four years in the valley. ⚾ **Kendall Williams**, Toronto's second-round pick in 2019, got nearly $150,000 over slot to spurn a commitment to Vanderbilt and hit the ground running in rookie ball with an unusually broad pitch mix (two fastballs, a curve, a slider and a change) for a starter of his age. ⚾ If **Josh Winckowski** continues his rapid ascent to the bump in Toronto, we could soon be following a Winck with a Giles, much to the delight of Harry Connick Jr fans everywhere. ⚾ He isn't the flashiest of former first-rounders, but **T.J. Zeuch** climbed to the majors despite striking out just a batter every other inning at Triple-A. Then again, one of those starts was a no-hitter in which the big right-hander struck out just three, so whatever works.

# Blue Jays Prospects

## The State of the System
Well, graduating two of the best prospects in baseball is going to leave a mark, but there's more depth here than you might have thought.

## The Top Ten

★ ★ ★ *2020 Top 101 Prospect* **#19** ★ ★ ★

**1. Nate Pearson  RHP**  OFP: 70  ETA: 2020
Born: 08/20/96  Age: 23  Bats: R  Throws: R  Height: 6'6"  Weight: 245
Origin: Round 1, 2017 Draft (#28 overall)

**The Report:** There hasn't been a pitching prospect since Noah Syndergaard that features this combination of overpowering stuff and physical imposition on the mound. After missing nearly the entire 2018 season, Pearson eclipsed the 100-inning mark for the first time in his career across three separate levels. It all starts with a top-of-the scale fastball that routinely touched triple-digits. Once the batter starts to cheat to catch up with 100+, he does a good job of reading swings and switching to the "slow" stuff. With the fastball having all the makings of a 70+ grade, his secondaries don't have to be perfect to be effective. His slider has very good late bite in the mid-to-upper 80s, while the changeup is very firm and still a work-in-progress. His power curveball comes from a tough release point, but is inconsistent.

The 2019 season couldn't have gone better for Pearson, whose innings were heavily monitored until the last month of the season. He proved he could ramp up his workload and stay healthy—even though previous injuries were more of the freak kind—and the stuff he displayed multiple times through the order put to bed the idea that a move to the bullpen was imminent. The next step is to continue working on his secondary pitches in 2020. There is effort to the delivery that could be cut down, but the overall physicality and strength of Pearson gives the appearance of a future workhorse in the top half of a rotation.

**Variance:** Medium. The stuff could play in the majors now, but there is always inherent risk with guys who throw as hard as Pearson.

**Ben Carsley's Fantasy Take:** Normally this would be the part of the program where I warn you against investing in fantasy pitching prospects, but Pearson is one of my dudes, and I'm in love. Yes, the risk is high, but Pearson offsets it by providing sky-high potential as well. It's all but a lock that Pearson will miss more than a bat per inning in whatever role he occupies, and despite his injury history, Pearson has the frame and athleticism required to log innings. If it all breaks right, we're looking at a bona fide SP1 who notches 200-plus Ks in 180-plus innings. But even a more moderate outcome should see Pearson rack up a ton of strikeouts. Sometimes you gotta jump in headfirst: I have Pearson as a top-25 dynasty prospect.

─────── ★ ★ ★ *2020 Top 101 Prospect* **#43** ★ ★ ★ ───────

**2** **Jordan Groshans  SS**          OFP: 60   ETA: 2022
Born: 11/10/99   Age: 20   Bats: R   Throws: R   Height: 6'3"   Weight: 205
Origin: Round 1, 2018 Draft (#12 overall)

**The Report:** A foot injury limited Groshans to 23 games in the Midwest League this season. Prior to going down, he was on his way to a breakout season slashing .337/.427/.482 in 83 at-bats. Big and strong, Groshans projects as a plus bat with above-average contact ability and power. He has a quick trigger at the plate that allows him to catch up to velocity and the power plays in-game to all fields. The Jays will continue to give him reps at shortstop, where he's average as a defender, but his defensive future is likely at third. He has the arm strength and instincts to be solid at the hot corner.

There wasn't much time to catch Groshans in action this year, but when he was on the field it was easy to forget he was a teenager in his first full professional season. Rather, he looked more like a polished, college bat. And he's already showing the kind of hit/power combo you'd look for in a middle-of-the-order hitter.

**Variance:** High. Groshans has fewer than 100 games under his belt and is likely to begin 2020 back in Low-A. He'll need to prove that he can hit against more advanced pitching, and that foot issues won't be a recurring problem in the pros.

**Ben Carsley's Fantasy Take:** The Blue Jays start off their list with two personal favorites of mine. I don't believe in Groshans' ability to stick at short, but I like pretty much everything else about the package, and the Jays have a strong track record when it comes to developing this type of talent. He got a ton of buzz last year so he's unlikely to be available in deeper dynasty leagues, but if you play in a shallower format or your leaguemates were asleep, now is the time to buy. He's already a very legitimate top-101 candidate.

─────── ★ ★ ★ *2020 Top 101 Prospect* **#83** ★ ★ ★ ───────

**3** **Alek Manoah  RHP**          OFP: 60   ETA: Late 2021
Born: 01/09/98   Age: 22   Bats: R   Throws: R   Height: 6'6"   Weight: 260
Origin: Round 1, 2019 Draft (#11 overall)

**The Report:** You might be able to drop Manoah in a big league pen right now on the strength of his fastball/slider combo. The fastball sits mid 90s and routinely bumps higher in short bursts. He also gets extension from his height and stride, so the pitch gets on batters in a hurry and makes for an uncomfortable experience in the box. You can't sit fastball here either, as Manoah's slider was one of the better breaking balls in the NCAA, a mid-80s two-plane beast. It should easily end up plus and that might even be a grade light when the smoke clears. His change remains a work-in-progress, with the usual caveat that he hasn't needed even an average one as an amateur.

Manoah is a large human and can struggle with his command at times due to his size and arm action. The delivery will need to be cleaned up some to keep him as a starter long term, as will the command and changeup. Hmm, this might be a true backend Top 101, mid-rotation starter or late inning reliever prospect.

**Variance:** Medium. Manoah arguably had the best present stuff in the 2019 draft class, and the fastball/slider combo gives him a reasonably attainable major league relief fallback. However, the profile comes with a fair bit of relief risk as well.

**Ben Carsley's Fantasy Take:** Anyone else getting big-time Alex Meyer vibes? I am getting big-time Alex Meyer vibes. You're better off taking a shot on a dude like Manoah than you are a safer back-end type with low upside, but in most cases you're probably better off taking a position player than Manoah. He'll be in the big mishmosh of pitchers we end up dropping off the top-101, listing in the honorable mentions, or referencing as "he'd be in the next 50" come formal rankings time. He should absolutely be owned if your league rosters 150-plus prospects, but I still think there's considerable reliever risk here.

**4**   **Eric Pardinho**   **RHP**     OFP: 55   ETA: 2022
Born: 01/05/01   Age: 19   Bats: R   Throws: R   Height: 5'10"   Weight: 155
Origin: International Free Agent, 2017

**The Report:** It's been over three years now since Pardinho was the toast of baseball as the 15-year-old Brazilian dominating the WBC qualifying round. He remains largely the same—preternaturally advanced for his age, but with a frame that limits his projectability. The Blue Jays handled him extraordinarily carefully after a spring elbow injury, holding off his debut until late June, limiting his pitch counts, giving him extra rest, and ultimately shutting him down a few weeks early. Unsurprisingly, he wasn't entirely sharp in the six weeks he was on the mound. There is plenty of time though, because Pardinho is an 18-year-old who already made it to full-season ball.

When right, he is about as advanced a teenager as you'll find. At his best, he'll slings the fastball in the low 90s, touching the mid 90s, although he was generally below peak velocity in his 2019 stint. His primary offspeed is a plus curve, and he's been working on improving his changeup and sharpening and distinguishing his slider. The command and pitchability profile is unusually strong for a teenager. This season raised some serious durability concerns in addition to the ones which were already present due to his slight size and frame. Pardinho might end up as something less than a full starting pitcher, but that's less of a knock than it used to be.

**Variance:** High. He's an 18-year-old who just missed half the season with an elbow injury, so the risk is pretty significant no matter how developed and advanced he is.

**Ben Carsley's Fantasy Take:** Pardinho is a fun story, but that doesn't necessarily make him a great fantasy prospect. In fact, he represents a subset of pitcher that I find is often overvalued in our game; the dreaded "advanced teenage arm." That's great and all, but people often tend to bake in further improvement for these types even though the primary thing that makes them special is their advanced pitchability for their age. None of this is to say Pardinho is devoid of upside, but he doesn't have enough of it for me to go all-in given the risks associated with the profile. Only proceed if your league rosters 200-plus prospects.

### 5. Simeon Woods Richardson   RHP      OFP: 55   ETA: 2022
Born: 09/27/00   Age: 19   Bats: R   Throws: R   Height: 6'3"   Weight: 210
Origin: Round 2, 2018 Draft (#48 overall)

**The Report:** Woods Richardson looks the part as a big power righty from the state of Texas and he has the stuff to match. He fires from a high slot with plus arm speed and goes right after hitters. The delivery has some effort, but he repeats it pretty well because of his premier athleticism. The fastball and curveball are potential plus pitches. The heater sits mid 90s in short bursts and can tick higher while settling low-to-mid 90s in longer outings. The pitch shows good life up and down the zone.

Woods Richardson pairs the fastball with a sharp, 12-to-6 breaking ball that spins tight and features strong bite, playing well off the high-slot fastball. The changeup is well behind, currently a show-me pitch with firmness and lack of feel. Arm speed is on his side with the changeup, and it could take big steps forward with further reps, but it'll be difficult to project too much by way of gains given his current release point. The safe call is late-inning reliever with two knockout pitches, but those who especially like Woods Richardson see a mid-rotation starter with a third pitch of some kind. Either way, it's obvious that he has the frame and stuff for impactful major-league innings.

**Variance:** High. The value can shoot upward with the development of a third pitch, but there's the strong likelihood of a reliever outcome.

**Ben Carsley's Fantasy Take:** Woods Richardson (seriously, how is there not a hyphen) is in the same general tier of prospect as Pardinho, but I actually prefer him for our purposes. The odds may be greater that he's a reliever, but they're also greater that he'll make an impact if he does stick as a starter, or that he'll close if shifted to the bullpen. Essentially, this isn't a terribly unique profile, but as far as guys with it go, I like Woods Richardson a fair amount.

### 6. Anthony Kay   LHP

OFP: 55   ETA: 2019
Born: 03/21/95   Age: 25   Bats: L   Throws: L   Height: 6'0"   Weight: 218
Origin: Round 1, 2016 Draft (#31 overall)

**The Report:** Now almost three full years off his post-draft Tommy John, Kay started to put it all together in 2019 and pitched well enough in the upper minors to get a cup of coffee with his new Canadian team. The fastball sits in the low 90s, bumping 95+ early in his outings. It will show hard, late run at times, but the overall command profile is a bit too much "wild in the zone." The changeup was his signature pitch in college, but it has been inconsistent post-surgery. Kay sells the offering well, but it's inconsistent and can show more as a straight change rather than as a true bat-misser. It will flash almost Wiffle ball arm-side movement at times, though, and should play as at least an average major league offering.

Kay has developed a much better curveball in the pros, a tight 1-7 yakker that tunnels well off the fastball. He also manipulates the speed of the pitch effectively—running from the mid 70s all the way up to 80—and can spot it to either side of the plate. The breaker can get a bit lazy at times, or show as more of a chase offering. More advanced hitters were able to lay off the curve once Kay got out of the Eastern League, but it still projects as an above-average offering that could get to plus with a bit more refinement.

Kay has three average-or-better pitches, more than enough to stick in the middle of a rotation, but he can struggle with both efficiency and strike-throwing. He may lack a true putaway pitch in the majors, and has had issues bleeding stuff after 50-60 pitches or so. But overall, he's a major-league-ready, polished lefty starting pitcher.

**Variance:** Low. There's some risk the breaker doesn't play as well in the majors as it did in Double-A and Kay is more of a five-and-dive fifth starter, but he's already seen big league time and has three average-or-better pitches in his arsenal.

**Ben Carsley's Fantasy Take:** Kay is a good name to file away if you're looking for some under-the-radar 2020 contributions in your very deep mixed or AL-only league. There's nothing in front of him in Toronto's rotation at present, and he's got enough skill to stick around as a No. 4/5 starter on a decent team. If you're hunting for a high-upside prospect, however, you can move along.

### 7. Gabriel Moreno   C

OFP: 55   ETA: 2022
Born: 02/14/00   Age: 20   Bats: R   Throws: R   Height: 5'11"   Weight: 160
Origin: International Free Agent, 2016

## Toronto Blue Jays 2020

**The Report:** Moreno is one of my favorite Midwest League bats of the year. He's slight—and is likely shorter than his listed height, but he's a big ball of energy on the field. His teammates seem to like him and feed off that energy, which is exactly what you want from a catcher. For me, he's more impressive at the plate than behind it, and the hit tool leads the way. The bat-to-ball skills are all there and the barrel control is impressive. His stance and swing are atypical with almost no weight transfer, but Moreno manages to show respectable power, and the ball jumps off his bat. As he advances, it will be interesting to see if he adds some weight transfer to his swing and how that affects his power and bat-to-ball skills. If the latter doesn't suffer with added lower-half movement, he may eventually tap into above-average game power.

Moreno is raw behind the plate and his arm is merely average. He does have a quick transfer though, so it is unlikely that the arm will force him out from behind the plate. At present he isn't a great receiver, but he's athletic and moves well behind the plate. Glovework for a catcher seems to be a teachable skill, so we will check on Moreno's progression in that dimension of his game down the road. There are decent foundational tools here already, though.

**Variance:** High. If he has to move from behind the plate, it's uncertain if the bat will carry the profile. If there is more power without sacrificing the hit tool, he might top that OFP.

**Ben Carsley's Fantasy Take:** Friends don't let friends draft fantasy catching prospects. That's especially true when said prospects aren't guaranteed to stick at catcher.

### 8  Orelvis Martinez   SS         OFP: 55   ETA: 2023
Born: 11/19/01   Age: 18   Bats: R   Throws: R   Height: 6'1"   Weight: 188
Origin: International Free Agent, 2018

**The Report:** The Blue Jays' biggest bonus baby in their 2018 J2 Class, Martinez looked the seven-figure part. At the plate he shows quality bat speed and uses the whole field to his advantage, showing advanced feel for hitting for someone so young. He is lean now but already shows average raw power, which should grow into potential plus raw power as he further matures, and he already shows big exit velocity with loft for a 17-year-old.

Defensively he may lose a step as he enters his twenties, pushing him off shortstop, but for now he combines good actions with plus arm strength and plus hands. He can be overly aggressive and flashy on the field, but these are things that iron out over time. The defensive tools would fit well at third base long term, and if the game power gets at least to plus, that bat will be more than enough to carry a corner.

**Variance:** High. While still young and having an impressive debut year, he could fill out the wrong way or see his aggression limit the hit tool. If/when he loses a step he could lose athleticism as well, moving him down the defensive spectrum.

**Ben Carsley's Fantasy Take:** Martinez is a total flier, but he's a fairly fun one as fliers go. Plus, he reminded me of Runelvys Hernandez, so overall I see this as a total win.

### 9. Josh Winckowski   RHP        OFP: 55   ETA: 2021
Born: 06/28/98   Age: 22   Bats: R   Throws: R   Height: 6'4"   Weight: 202
Origin: Round 15, 2016 Draft (#462 overall)

**The Report:** Winckowski has been steadily moving up the organizational ladder since being drafted in 2016, but had a breakout season this year in A-ball. He gets good extension on his heavy fastball, which sits in the mid 90s with late life. The changeup works well off of the heater and is a potential swing-and-miss pitch. Winckowski replicates his arm action well and the pitch shows good arm-side fade. His slider is inconsistent and can lack depth, but has an average projection. Physically, he's got the classic starter's build and if the secondaries develop he would profile as an innings eater at the back of the rotation.

**Variance:** High. Needs to get a bit more out of the breaking ball to reach his OFP and hasn't pitched in the upper minors yet.

**Ben Carsley's Fantasy Take:** A low-ceiling pitcher with high risk who's not ready right now: sign me up! Just kidding. Please do not sign me up. In fact, please remove me from your email list.

### 10. Griffin Conine   OF        OFP: 50   ETA: 2022
Born: 07/11/97   Age: 22   Bats: L   Throws: R   Height: 6'1"   Weight: 200
Origin: Round 2, 2018 Draft (#52 overall)

**The Report:** After missing the first 50 games of the season due to a positive test for a banned stimulant, Conine arrived in the Midwest League, showing off the plus raw power that made him a potential first-round pick in 2018. The power does come with a cost at the plate, though, as his strikeout rate in Low-A was over 35 percent. Defensively, he's limited to a corner spot where he makes up for below-average range with good instincts. He'll be able to hold down right field with an arm that's accurate and strong. Conine has the makings of a classic power hitting right-fielder but he'll need to tighten up the approach at the plate to reach that profile.

**Variance:** High. There are questions about whether the hit tool will play and Conine has yet to face advanced pitching.

## Toronto Blue Jays 2020

**Ben Carsley's Fantasy Take:** On the one hand, Conine doesn't have a terribly exciting fantasy profile. On the other hand, he's the son of a former big leaguer in Toronto's system, so he's probably at least a role-60 player in disguise. Add him to your watch list, but don't pounce yet.

## The Next Ten

### 11 Adam Kloffenstein   RHP
Born: 08/25/00   Age: 19   Bats: R   Throws: R   Height: 6'5"   Weight: 243
Origin: Round 3, 2018 Draft (#88 overall)

Kloffenstein wasn't all that different a draft prospect from his now org-mate Woods Richardson. He went a round later last summer, but commanded a bigger bonus to buy him out of his college commitment. He's your more traditional "everything's bigger in Texas" prep arm, a towering, physically mature 6'5" even while playing almost the entire year at age 18. But while Woods Richardson's stuff popped in A-ball, Kloffenstein sat more low 90s—as opposed to the mid 90s he flashed his draft year—and the profile looked more strike-thrower than big stuff guy. As mentioned, he just turned 19, and it's an ideal starter's frame, but he might not be as safe a prep arm as we posited last year, which is still risky, but now riskier.

### 12 Alejandro Kirk   C
Born: 11/06/98   Age: 21   Bats: R   Throws: R   Height: 5'9"   Weight: 220
Origin: International Free Agent, 2016

Kirk will undoubtedly draw comparisons to Willians Astudillo for a handful of reasons. They are both international catchers with rather large, not jean-modeling frames, they rarely swing and miss, they get on base, and while the former had been overlooked for some time, that is not the case with Kirk anymore. It isn't pretty sometimes. The bat speed doesn't wow you, the power isn't over the fence variety, he can't run, and you wouldn't be remiss if you didn't like the overall athleticism. He just gets on base and hits and hits. The swing works. It is short and direct to the ball, he recognizes pitches well, and he doesn't often force himself to swing at pitches out of the zone. The defense is better than you would imagine, as he blocks well, has tick-above-average arm strength, and has worked hard to improve his receiving. The overall outcome is a hit over power, on-base driven catcher. The risk here is that if he stops getting on-base there isn't anything else to carry the load, but hey was this even a profile you would have banked on even just a few years ago?

### 13 T.J. Zeuch   RHP
Born: 08/01/95   Age: 24   Bats: R   Throws: R   Height: 6'7"   Weight: 225
Origin: Round 1, 2016 Draft (#21 overall)

Zeuch is probably going to pitch in the majors for a long time. It's a bushel of average or slightly-above pitches. He leads off with a sinker that typically sits 91-94, topping out at 95, and rides in with plus movement especially against righties. He'll also show you a slider, a curve, and a change that all come in around average and flash higher. That stuff from a 6'7" pitcher with a classic delivery explains the "former first-round pick" part pretty easily. Yet the sum as a professional pitcher has, to date, been less than the sum of his parts. He just hasn't fooled enough batters to strike anyone out despite being an advanced college pitcher with, what is on paper, pretty good stuff. He came up for September and was fine, used as both a back-end starter and the bulk guy behind an opener. He currently profiles as, well, pretty much that moving forward, with an asterisk denoting that tall pitchers with good stuff are more likely to suddenly put it together quite late in the development cycle.

## 14 Kendall Williams   RHP
Born: 08/24/00   Age: 19   Bats: R   Throws: R   Height: 6'6"   Weight: 205
Origin: Round 2, 2019 Draft (#52 overall)

In yesteryear's baseball, a player like Williams probably gets drafted much higher, and ends up much higher on prospect lists. Who doesn't like a 6'6" right-hander who showed an above-average fastball and potential plus curveball? He was simply too much for young hitters in the complex given his size, angle, strike throwing, and stuff. The stuff is still inconsistent and the fastball dropped later in the year as he wore down, which was partially why he was still on the board at 52. Williams's stuff should be ready for a full-season roster next year, but they will most likely keep him in extended to add strength to his wiry frame.

## 15 Dasan Brown   OF
Born: 09/25/01   Age: 18   Bats: R   Throws: R   Height: 6'0"   Weight: 185
Origin: Round 3, 2019 Draft (#88 overall)

A local kid whom the Jays drafted out of an Ontario high school, Brown displays a collection of loud tools. At the plate, he shows plus raw power. While his understanding of the zone is advanced for the age, his pitch recognition is undeveloped and, consequently, there are a lot of whiffs, especially against offspeed stuff. The swing itself comes with length. The arm and speed (which is plus to plus-plus) are sufficient for him to stick in center, though he may have to slide to a corner at physical maturity. There's a major-league regular ceiling here, but his road to The Show will be longer than a Dream Theater song.

## 16 Miguel Hiraldo   IF
Born: 09/05/00   Age: 19   Bats: R   Throws: R   Height: 5'11"   Weight: 170
Origin: International Free Agent, 2017

## Toronto Blue Jays 2020

Hiraldo, a $750k bonus baby out of the Dominican in 2017, has some thunder in his stick. The bat is going to have to carry the profile here, as he's already playing a lot of second base, and his arm is likely to limit him there in the medium-to-long term, and the glove isn't much more than average even at the keystone. There might be enough juice in the offensive profile to make it work though, as a potential average hit/solid-average power combo isn't hard to see. And Hiraldo will spend all of next season as a 19-year-old. He's definitely a potential breakout Blue Jays name for 2020.

### 17 Otto Lopez  SS
Born: 10/01/98   Age: 21   Bats: R   Throws: R   Height: 5'10"   Weight: 160
Origin: International Free Agent, 2016

The Jays seem to be grooming Lopez for a super utility role. This year most of his reps came at short, but he has played everywhere but first and catcher during his professional career. He is more than capable at short, but that position may be occupied in Toronto for a while. Lopez is a clean, smooth defender with good footwork, hands, and body control. At the plate he's balanced and takes confident swings. He doesn't strike out much thanks to quick hands, a simple, smooth swing, and a flat bat path that's relatively short to the ball. He really doesn't do anything poorly, but he's not flashy and aside from the hit tool, he lacks any other loud aspect to his game. He's never going to be a top prospect, but expect him to continue putting up strong batting averages until he cracks the majors. If things go well developmentally he may wind up an everyday player. There isn't a lot of variance in his profile, so the floor is high here.

### 18 Riley Adams  C
Born: 06/26/96   Age: 24   Bats: R   Throws: R   Height: 6'4"   Weight: 225
Origin: Round 3, 2017 Draft (#99 overall)

A third-round pick in the 2017 draft, Adams conquered the Florida State League on his second go-around and was perfectly fine over a half-season-plus in New Hampshire. The profile behind the plate is a bit nondescript if I'm honest. He's much taller and a bit narrower than your average catcher, but he's reasonably quiet and athletic behind the dish, although he can snatch for the low strike. There's a solid approach at the plate, but some stiffness to the swing that leads to swing-and-miss in the zone, although it gives him potential above-average pop as well. This was the kind of catcher that was a backup for a decade in the late-90s or early-00s. A passable glove that could run into a bomb for you. With the modern emphasis on receiving, Adams might have a tougher time getting major league per diems, but the profile is still solid backup catcher on balance.

### 19 Patrick Murphy  RHP
Born: 06/10/95   Age: 25   Bats: R   Throws: R   Height: 6'4"   Weight: 220
Origin: Round 3, 2013 Draft (#83 overall)

The early part of Murphy's pro career was routinely interrupted by injuries, but he was healthy and showing progress throughout 2018 and early 2019. That all came to a screeching halt last summer when his delivery was deemed illegal by the Major League Baseball Umpires Association, and he was sent back to the drawing board to craft a new set of mechanics that removed his key timing mechanism—a toe tap just before he began his drive toward the plate. Prior to that revelation, Murphy was consistently showing a plus fastball and plus curveball with potential for impact in the middle-to-late innings out of the bullpen. Now, after only throwing 20 innings in the season's final three months following news of his illegal delivery, Murphy's future is decidedly up in the air. Any challenges finding consistency with his new mechanics could hasten an already-likely move to the bullpen, and the timeline for his big league debut could be pushed back beyond 2020.

### 20 Kevin Smith SS
Born: 07/04/96  Age: 23  Bats: R  Throws: R  Height: 5'11"  Weight: 188
Origin: Round 4, 2017 Draft (#129 overall)

We ranked Smith in the top five of last year's list based on his quick hands and above-average bat speed. We had hope for a good offensive outcome despite some continuing pitch recognition and approach issues, and he performed well at the A-ball levels. He proceeded to hit .209 with a 32 percent strikeout rate in Double-A in 2019, and then followed it up by performing about as well as your random American League pitcher in interleague at the plate in the Arizona Fall League. Worse, he looked just as lost as those numbers indicate. There's enough of an excuse with a failed swing change that tried to tap into his raw—and help him deal better with the high fastballs that he's always struggled against—to hope that some of this comes back around. And there's always the utility fallback for a versatile player who can handle the 6, of course. But we really didn't see or hear a single good thing on his bat out of the Eastern League or the Arizona Fall League all year.

## Personal Cheeseball

### PC Jordan Romano RHP
Born: 04/21/93  Age: 27  Bats: R  Throws: R  Height: 6'4"  Weight: 200
Origin: Round 10, 2014 Draft (#294 overall)

I've liked Romano for some time as a late-blooming arm of interest, in that sort of way that you like 45 OFP future relievers sometimes. I wasn't surprised to see him get a shot with the Rangers in last year's Rule 5 Draft; arms who can both potentially contribute now and have some projection are the prototypical Rule 5 picks. He was returned to the Toronto system late in spring training, but got called up in June and promptly touched 100 in his major league debut. That's a bit above where he typically pitches, and surely he was jazzed up for his first game in the majors, but he does sit 94-96 regularly. He pairs the fastball with a decent little hard slider, having dropped a not-so-hot change since becoming a reliever. He's definitionally a 95-and-a-slider pen guy, but it's always fun to see a random arm out of nowhere who you pegged at that outcome actually get there.

## Low Minors Sleeper

**LMS**

**Alejandro Melean    RHP**
Born: 10/11/00   Age: 19   Bats: R   Throws: R   Height: 6'0"   Weight: 175
Origin: International Free Agent, 2017

Part of the '17 J2 class, Melean doesn't have ideal size as he is smaller than the 6-foot, 175 pounds listed on his player card, but he still has quality stuff. Melean features a fastball that sits in the low 90s, touching higher with quality sink, and a slider that has flashed for me in the past. This past season was a bit of a lost one for the right-hander, though, as he battled various injuries and had control issues. On the positive side he finished his second year of pro ball and got out of the complex before turning 19. Look for this young arm to rebound next season with improved health.

## Top Talents 25 and Under (as of 4/1/2020)

1. Vladimir Guerrero Jr.
2. Bo Bichette
3. Nate Pearson
4. Jordan Groshans
5. Cavan Biggio
6. Alek Manoah
7. Eric Pardinho
8. Danny Jansen
9. Simeon Woods Richardson
10. Anthony Kay

Guerrero Jr. didn't light the world aflame during his much-anticipated debut. He merely sparked a match, putting up league-average offense while oftentimes giving us a taste of his prodigious power (the Home Run Derby doesn't count but, ya know, it was still cool). He did it at the age of 20 and will play the entirety of his sophomore season at the age of 21. Nothing he did or did not do in his first season leads us to believe he's anything less than what was expected of him when he was the No. 1 prospect in all of baseball a year ago.

The player Vladito is expected to stand next to on the infield for the next half-decade or so came up later in the season but was arguably just as impressive. Bichette's raw power played up in games and he showed an advanced hit tool. He's not likely to contend for any fielding awards at the 6 but can hold his own over there. So much of the Blue Jays' future depends on Guerrero Jr. and Bichette living up to expectations, and they're off to a solid start.

The third and least-heralded of the Major League Sons, Biggio, was actually the most productive in his 430-plate appearance sample after ranking just 11th in the system a year ago. Biggio looked the part of the TTO utility infielder many projected him to be, showing an advanced eye that led to an OBP 130 points higher than his batting average. All told, he homered, walked, or struck out in 49 percent of his plate appearances and his 112 DRC+ was the best of the trio. Biggio's the oldest of the three by a good three years and has the lowest ceiling, thus his ranking a few spots down, but he proved at the very least to be a competent major leaguer.

Jansen was Example #206,754 that catchers are weird, as the bespectacled one came up as a potential bat-first power threat with a questionable glove and looked...like a solid defender with a questionable hit tool. He finished with the seventh best CDA (Catcher Defensive Adjustment) in baseball, which was almost entirely the reason behind his 2.2 WARP. Catching development remains unpredictable, but the defense at the very least should afford him more opportunities to snatch the starting gig long term.

# Part 3: Featured Articles

# The Baseball Is Juiced (Again)

## Robert Arthur

*This article originally appeared at Baseball Prospectus on April 5, 2019.*

It started when the normally reliable Chris Sale got lit up for three homers by the Mariners in the Red Sox's season opener. It was part of a record number of taters that flew on Opening Day, as starters from Sale to Zack Greinke were taken deep by the handful. Then Christian Yelich hit a home run in each of his first four games, tying yet another MLB record, this one for consecutive games with a dinger to start a season.

It didn't take long for fans and players to begin whispering and tweeting about the baseballs being juiced again. It's early yet for us to come to any definitive conclusion about the 2019 season, but preliminary data shows that the baseball has returned to its aerodynamic peak. Whether that means this season will smash home run records like 2017 did remains to be seen.

Before home run explosion over the last few years, no one worried too much about the baseball's air resistance. While MLB and Rawlings (the company that manufactures the official baseballs) kept track of dozens of metrics to make sure that the ball was consistent from month to month, they didn't measure drag.

But drag is incredibly important in determining how likely a hitter is to knock one out of the park. As baseballs become more aerodynamic, they travel further given a certain initial velocity. A deep fly ball that might have been caught at the warning track can instead go into the first row of the stands. A three percent change in drag coefficient can work to add about five feet to a well-hit fly ball, which can in turn increase home runs league wide by an astounding 10-15 percent.

It's possible to measure the aerodynamics of the baseball using the pitch-tracking radars currently in place in each MLB ballpark. By calculating the loss of speed from when the pitch is released to when it crosses the plate, you can directly measure the drag coefficient on the baseball. I first wrote about the role of decreasing drag in boosting home runs in 2017, and MLB's commission of scientists and statisticians later confirmed that the more aerodynamic baseballs in use that year were largely to blame for the spike in home runs. The same commission rejected some alternate hypotheses, like rising temperatures and a league-wide boost in launch angle pushing more balls over the fence.

The current era has featured some large fluctuations in drag coefficient, leading to first an explosion in 2016 and 2017, and then a dialing back of homers last year. Curious about the record-breaking home run tallies in the last few days, I used the same methodology to measure the aerodynamics of the baseballs so far in 2019.

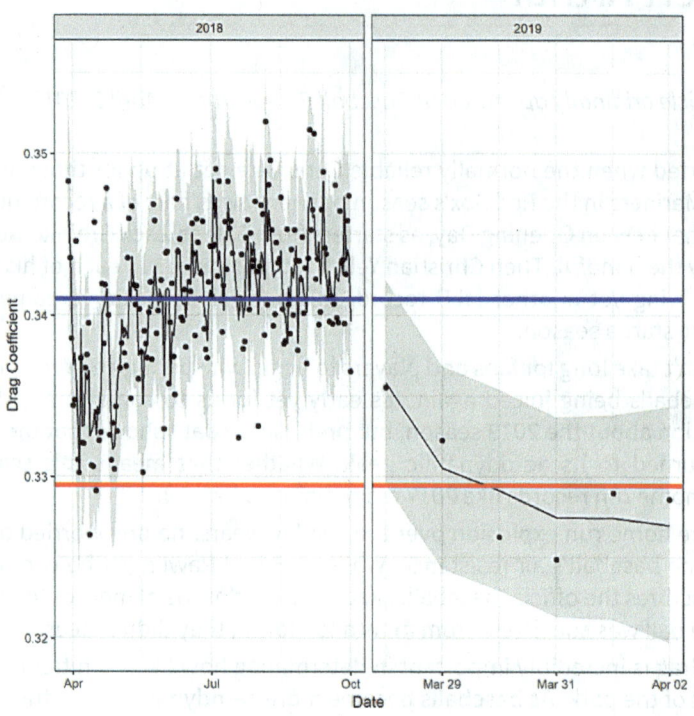

We're only a week into the 2019 season, but the drag numbers so far are among the lowest recorded in the last calendar year. With apologies for gory math, the current 2019 season average drag coefficient (the red line) would be below the 95 percent credible interval (the shaded area) for about nine-tenths of the 2018 season. (I used a Bayesian Random Walk model implemented in INLA to calculate these credible intervals, averaging the drag numbers in each game and adjusting for park.)

There were only a handful of six-day stretches in 2018 that had drag numbers below what we're seeing now, and most were in late June and early July. All of this means that 2019's data so far is quite a bit different than what we saw through most of last year.

These drag coefficients factor out the effects of temperature and air density, so they aren't a product of April cold. However, the numbers could be deceptive if the radars used to track pitches have changed from year to year. I consulted with some experts within baseball who were not aware of any specific modifications to the radar this year that could produce this pattern, but it's an important caveat of which to be aware.

On the one hand, it's only been six days, and we don't quite have the statistical basis to say that these drag coefficients are unprecedented compared to 2018. On the other hand, we've witnessed about 5,000 fastballs so far this season, so it's not as if our sample size is small. At least so far, the baseball has played like it's much more aerodynamic than it was last year. In fact, the current drag coefficient is really only comparable to 2017, when the baseballs were more aerodynamic than they had been in at least a decade.

It's not just fancy radar tracking indicating that the baseball is flying through the air more easily. The current number of home runs per game (as of this writing) is the highest it's been since the heady days of 2017, the year that teams and players broke dinger-related records everywhere you looked. That's especially remarkable considering that we're in what is typically the coldest part of the regular season, when lower temperatures and higher winds tend to suppress offense and keep balls in the air within the park. Comparing only from April to April, this year's rate of home runs per fly ball is even a little bit higher than it was in 2017.

With that said, the current measurements are no guarantee that 2019 will be another year of record-shattering homer hitting. The trouble with the drag measurements is that they are not consistent from June to August, from week to week, or even sometimes from day to day. Whether because of natural manufacturing variation or differences in the underlying supplies of cowhide and thread that go into the baseballs, drag has a tendency to fluctuate up and down over the course of a year. So the homers that fly in the first week of April wouldn't necessarily clear the fence a week later.

It's possible that this one-week drop in drag coefficient subsides and the baseball returns to its 2018 levels. On the other hand, it's almost equally probable that the ball becomes even more slippery and flies ever farther. Either way, it's clear that the baseball's air resistance is something to keep an eye on for the remainder of the 2019 season.

—*Robert Arthur is an author of Baseball Prospectus.*

# The Moral Hazard of Playing It Safe

## Craig Goldstein

*This article originally appeared at Baseball Prospectus on August 6, 2019.*

A couple days prior to the trade deadline, amidst a sea of tranquility posing as the lead up to the trade deadline, Bob Nightengale took to Twitter. Nightengale, who was probably wearing his pants backwards at the time, tweeted that MLB GMs were coming around on the idea that the unified trade deadline should be moved back from July 31 to August 15, so they could better assess their positions in the standings and whether they should buy or sell. To which I said:

This might strike some as reductive and churlish. And it might be that, but it isn't really wrong, either. Jeff Quinton wrote a great piece discussing the environmental factors that enable front offices to avoid risk without upsetting the apple cart within their own fanbases. I don't believe that it goes far enough, however. His article gives us the proper framework through which to understand why these behaviors have been allowed to seep into front offices throughout the league. Understanding the reasons behind these actions are different from excusing them, though, and GMs should not be let off the hook for their non-competitive approach to the trade deadline (much less the offseason).

⚾ ⚾ ⚾

It's fair to say that fans as a group have rarely, if ever, been pro-player. It is also fair to say that in the time during and following the Moneyball revolution, the pendulum swung from fans who cared intensely about winning in the moment (and thus might be intolerant of a rebuilding approach) to fans who supported building a team that could compete throughout multiple seasons, viewing the playoffs as a crapshoot, with the thought that getting multiple bites at the apple was a better approach than taking a bigger bite in any one season.

There's nothing wrong with that approach, and I still find merit in that argument. However, it seems that the pendulum has swung too far in that direction. Teams are overvaluing some of the individual factors that make themselves long-term contenders rather than attempting to seize a championship when given the opportunity. It's a difficult needle to thread.

And surely, they (and those in similar positions) would have liked another two weeks to clarify where they stand so as to better marshal their resources. We've all asked for a few more minutes when staring at a menu. But all of these GMs and front office personnel are where they are to make difficult decisions. They have proprietary data and internal analysts dedicated to understanding their position relative to the rest of the league, and how any move in the here and now impacts their long-term vision. To complain (if that report is accurate) that over half the season is not enough to properly assess their season is bullshit of the highest order. Move the deadline, and you'd simply have increasingly discounted trade offers because teams would be acquiring even less control of anyone they're acquiring, rental or not.

Major league front offices are behaving like the managers they lampooned two decades ago. They're effectively sacrificing a runner to second in the ninth inning—not because it's the correct move, but rather because it is safe. It used to be that the phrase "moral hazard" was used to describe general managers who made ill-fated, short-sighted decisions aimed at locking in wins and securing their jobs at the expense of their team's future. Now, general managers are guilty of committing moral hazards in the opposite direction, playing it utterly safe and terrified of becoming scapegoats.

In lieu of bold action, they opt to pussyfoot around a current window of contention, choosing instead to play the long game and stack up years of control like they're blocks in a game of Jenga. GMs pass on signing quality players in free agency because the back-end of the deal might look bad, and because they might be able to squeeze out 70 percent of the production from a player who costs a tenth as much. That's a safer investment, too, because it's also hard to prove a negative—it's impossible to prove that Manny Machado would make the Mets a playoff team in 2019-2020, but it's easy to say that the back half of Robinson Cano's contract sucks. Owners, who rule over GM's jobs, are also humans with human brain processes that will always make the so-called albatross contract uglier than the road not taken.

These days, GMs are remembered for the bad deals they make and the surplus value they generate, not the acquisition of expensive, necessary talents that meet their market worth (or fall slightly short while still providing significant on-field value). And front offices know that one or two expensive misfires can cost them their jobs, no matter how many good deals they make.

No front office exemplifies this ethos more than the Toronto Blue Jays. General Manager Ross Atkins had this to say following the Blue Jays underwhelming trade deadline:

This is by no means the first time that an executive will cite years of control to justify their actions, which is often just another way of saying "don't look at what we got, look at how much we got of it." Atkins touts quantity to elide the discussion of quality—either, that of the players acquired, or those given up. Remember: the other teams presumably value years of control, too.

Atkins also had some thoughts to offer regarding free agents back in early 2018:

This ignores, of course, whether the player can create enough value in the front end of a contract to justify the longer term of a deal, and the decline that often occurs in the back end. It also ignores whether the player can fill a need the team requires and put them in a position to compete for and win a championship. But as teams seemingly avoid contention at all, where they might end up having to consider and later justify some of these tough decisions, we still see risk-averse approaches.

Anthony Fenech's article on two trades that recently extended GM Al Avila didn't make got at this issue rather well:

> Passing on those deals was defensible: Both players had yet to break out and trading [Michael] Fulmer—a pitcher who appeared to be a future ace, no matter his injury concerns—would have taken serious gumption, opening Avila up to strong criticism.

Avoiding strong criticism is something each of us can understand as a motivation, but the avoidance of criticism only matters if that criticism is valid. In Fulmer's case, shoving his injury concerns aside affects not only the years that the team controls him (he is currently missing a full season due to Tommy John surgery) but also the quality of those seasons, as his knee and elbow injuries combined to dampen his effectiveness even when healthy enough to pitch. But it was easy to present the then-current image of Fulmer as a top of the rotation pitcher who the team had under its domain for the next five seasons as something to build around. The status quo isn't nearly as often second-guessed as a decision that disrupts it.

⚾ ⚾ ⚾

MLB GMs are risk-averse to a fault. They are ivy-educated and consulting firm-approved, and yet they can't seem to avoid leaving wins on the table in their all-consuming lust for a non-existent $/WAR championship. They are supposed to zig when everyone else zags, and not merely pay lip service to the idea of zigging through a calculated PR plan built on convincing the fan base their approach is novel when it actually apes most of their competitors. Instead they've become far more concerned with making safe, accepted-by-the-new-common-wisdom decisions, such that our prior understanding of what a moral hazard is has become inverted.

I can't blame them entirely, and not only because of the reasons that Quinton illuminated in his article, but also because of the damage wrought by the introduction of the second wild card (WC2) spot. MLB's desire to have more teams in playoff contention has sparked anti-competitive behavior. Teams know now that they do not need to swing big as they assemble their roster because there is a good chance that a mediocre team can either catch fire and capture a division, or muddle along until they back into the WC2.

Simultaneously, the one-game playoff has neutered the WC1, putting an entire season on the flip of a coin like some sort of baseball-obsessed Anton Chigurh. While the one-game playoff makes sense as a way to increase the value of winning a division, it also means that if a front office doesn't like its chances of overcoming a behemoth like the Dodgers or Astros in the offseason, they have few incentives to chase glory. Similarly, the relative inaction in the NL Central at the trade deadline—despite a wide open division—can be explained by the idea that any high-variance investment could still result in only a wild card (or worse) result, given the mere two months left in the season to make an impact.

⚾ ⚾ ⚾

As stated at the top, we should not confuse reasons for excuses. The implementation of the second wild card is just one of many environmental factors that influence how each front office operates. I am convinced that it is one of the larger factors, but I am also convinced that organizations need to shed the yoke of "efficiency at all costs" so that they can instead pursue competition, as the spirit of the game intends. Until they do, we're all deadline losers.

—*Craig Goldstein is an author of Baseball Prospectus.*

# Index of Names

| | | | |
|---|---|---|---|
| Adams, Riley | 110 | Hiraldo, Miguel | 96, 109 |
| Alford, Anthony | 96 | Jansen, Danny | 35 |
| Anderson, Chase | 47 | Jimenez, Leonardo | 96 |
| Bass, Anthony | 49 | Johnston, Kyle | 98 |
| Bergen, Travis | 98 | Kay, Anthony | 61, 105 |
| Bichette, Bo | 18 | Kingham, Nick | 98 |
| Biggio, Cavan | 20 | Kirk, Alejandro | 96, 108 |
| Borucki, Ryan | 90 | Kloffenstein, Adam | 91, 108 |
| Boshers, Buddy | 51 | Lopez, Otto | 110 |
| Brown, Dasan | 109 | Luciano, Elvis | 63 |
| Buchholz, Clay | 53 | Manoah, Alek | 92, 102 |
| Castillo, Maximo | 98 | Martinez, Orelvis | 87, 106 |
| Cole, A.J. | 98 | Mayza, Tim | 65 |
| Conine, Griffin | 85, 107 | McClelland, Jackson | 98 |
| Davis, Jonathan | 96 | McGuire, Reese | 37 |
| Diaz, Yennsy | 98 | McKinney, Billy | 39 |
| Drury, Brandon | 22 | Melean, Alejandro | 112 |
| Dull, Ryan | 98 | Miller, Justin | 98 |
| Espinal, Santiago | 96 | Moran, Brian | 67 |
| Feierabend, Ryan | 98 | Moreno, Gabriel | 96, 105 |
| Fisher, Derek | 24 | Murphy, Patrick | 98, 110 |
| Font, Wilmer | 55 | Panik, Joe | 41 |
| Gaviglio, Sam | 57 | Pannone, Thomas | 69 |
| Giles, Ken | 59 | Pardinho, Eric | 93, 103 |
| Grichuk, Randal | 26 | Pearson, Nate | 94, 101 |
| Groshans, Jordan | 86, 102 | Perez, Hector | 98 |
| Guerrero Jr., Vladimir | 28 | Rees, Jackson | 98 |
| Gurriel Jr., Lourdes | 31 | Reid-Foley, Sean | 71 |
| Hanson, Alen | 96 | Richard, Clayton | 98 |
| Hatch, Thomas | 98 | Roark, Tanner | 73 |
| Hernández, Teoscar | 33 | Romano, Jordan | 75, 111 |

Toronto Blue Jays 2020

| | | | |
|---|---|---|---|
| Ryu, Hyun-Jin | 77 | Valera, Breyvic | 96 |
| Shaw, Travis | 43 | Waguespack, Jacob | 83 |
| Shoemaker, Matt | 79 | Wall, Forrest | 96 |
| Smith, Kevin | 88, 111 | Williams, Kendall | 99, 109 |
| Stewart, Brock | 98 | Winckowski, Josh | 99, 107 |
| Taylor, Samad | 96 | Woods Richardson, Simeon | 95, 104 |
| Tejada, Rubén | 89 | Yamaguchi, Shun | 96 |
| Tellez, Rowdy | 45 | Young, Chavez | 96 |
| Thornton, Trent | 81 | Zeuch, T.J. | 99, 108 |